I0741497

Dedicated to Don and Jody:
"Love like endless rain."

All fiction is fiction; all nonfiction is not, but not about you; and all poetry is mined from imagination.

APRIL GLOAMING

Publisher's Cataloging-in-Publication Data

Umenhofer, Lance
The regenerates II/edited by Lance Umenhofer/
designed by Drew Holden
ISBN 978-0-9882061-2-0

1. Poetry: General 2. Fiction: General
3. Literary Collections: General

Library of Congress Control Number: 2016908461

THE REGENERATES II
REVIVAL
An Anthology of 12 Southern Artists Through the Eyes of 12 Southern Authors

Edited and Compiled by:
Lance Umenhofer
Collection Designed by:
Drew Holden

THE REGENERATES

Even before the events of 1861–65, before Rosecrans burned Nashville, before Sherman razed Atlanta, before Grant pummeled Richmond, the South could never really be described as a bastion of culture and progress. It was a more exaggerated, obverse reflection of what it is now: a society of far-spread poor, without much of an education, and who, on average, would marry younger and die sooner than their northern counterparts.

Southerners are the grotesque caricature of what it means to be American. We are the hillbilly, the redneck, the inbred. We marry our cousins and write 'Jesus' on our voting ballots. We bring snakes to church and let them bite us so that we might prove God to ourselves. We are the slough-faced bloodhound baying next to the majestic greyhound (our 'brother'). We are the embarrassing family secret, the beyond-lost cause, the expendable limb. We are also the land of Faulkner and Poe, of Welty and O'Conner, of Capote and Carothers and McCarthy. We consistently produce some of the best measuring sticks for literary achievement. From Twain to Dubus, from Toole to Wright. A Southern artist is both born and made. And always immediately recognizable.

The Southern artist is oppressively aware of her essence, of the paradox of herself and her surroundings.

She is an outcast in an already outcast society, a double-jeopardy. Unlike most great artists, the Southern artist in particular produces work not for the people around her (because to them it is superfluous and ugly, they are too close to it) but for the ones outside of it. Whether that distance is spanned by space or time or both, the Southern artist must scream louder than the others in order to be heard.

Artists and Authors: The Regenerates are attempting to capture the screams of those who have lost their voices. It's about screaming so hard that the voice, the sound itself, becomes so full and powerful that it turns into light. It is about a collaboration of the visual and the oral, about the embodiment of sound and light. We will pair a Southern author with a Southern artist so that we might illuminate ourselves and find our own paradox—the particular paradox of being from the South, but also the paradox that goes beyond geography, beyond humanity, beyond even the luminous spark of consciousness.

We will ride the Mobius of self-discovery, the self-same plane of art that is the highway to ourselves, past ourselves, then back again. When it's done, what will we find?

REVIVAL

"The coming revival must begin with a great revival of [the arts]. It is in the closet, with the door shut, that the sound of abundance of rain will first be heard. An increase of secret [creation among artists, writers, and music] will be the sure harbinger of [equality and soul.]"

The Southern experience, and therefore, the southerner, is oftentimes looked at as lesser:

less educated,
less talented,
less loved,
less progressive,
less understood,

and less capable of creation beyond the typical scope, but why would this be? In a time where it has become well understood that from oppression, isolation, and an eye that has been shaped with iron, diamond cut saws, bits of string, an oyster knife, a broken pencil that is still trying to erase history, and impossible odds is how truly human art and connection can become a force mightier than the pen, stronger then the page and canvas. It can become the breath of a conversation that changes the perspective of the blind, and the weak, the restrained and unforgiven, the closeted and the strange, the lost and the found, the native and the immigrant.

The Regenerates are a collective of thinkers and dreamers that see Nashville for the truly brilliant and devastating landscape it is and want to paint the walls, write poetry on the streets, and hug and kiss our neighbors in this grotesque bazaar.

CLOSED MOUTHS
BY

Stephen Mage
(Interpreting Bobby Becker)

Threats linger by way of the weather in this area.

Our view from the steps shows the yard and the main road and the field that runs a half-mile to the hills. From the right angle, the telephone lines match the horizon. When sitting on the steps, I used to imagine the lines cutting clouds open over the hills and spilling the weather over them. You can watch it move, the weather, the wind and the rain, turning the leaves and grasses over to show their lighter greens, carrying something with them. Virgil would watch the weather with me. He loved the lone dogwood growing in the yard. You could watch the wind carry to the yard and the tree and he'd light up with the tree. I used to take him outside to look at the tree. Then he saw the lines and was scared and froze on the steps. The grass in the yard is long now.

We were sitting, us three, at the front door watching the storm move in over the hills.

Virg had his nose and cheeks all squished up against the glass so it fogged and he couldn't see out anymore. Jim pulled him back and wiped the fog with his sleeve, but Virg just pressed up to it again, and soon let go. Jim stood right behind and over him and the steam from his coffee fogged up his part of the glass too, and he wiped it and laughed and soon we were all laughing, though surely Virg had no idea why. It made me happy to see him laughing, on account of him only laughing when Jim laughed, and then only when the laughter was real.

When the wind reached the yard the tree there began shaking and the telephone lines too. Virgil took then to pressing his hands up against the glass and clawing at it. I crouched down to his level where he didn't notice and tried to see what he was reaching for. He had his eyes set firmly on the shaking tree. Jim saw too that Virg was looking at the tree and said, 'it's just trying to play catch with the wind,' but Virg paid the joke no mind.

• •

When Jim woke up we did rejoice; five months of no movement and of him gripping at his bed sheets brought everyone in the ward to silence. We expected noise if not speech, but when his eyes opened there was only his breathing, a scratching quicker than when he slept. No moan or gurgle or cough. None since before he was sent to his knees in the first place. But he clawed at the sheets with all of his old strength, gripping and twisting them. His eyes were wide open too, looking all around but not at us. His pupils grew and shrank with his breathing.

Once when he'd twisted the sheets nearly off of him, one of the nurses thought to maybe put something in his hands and brought a stress ball, and with a little bit of struggle, pried his fingers off the sheets and around it, to which he squeezed it until his nails dug into his palms and the stress ball was a pile of fabric all over him. His hands fell back to the sheets. He gripped a little less hard when Virgil brought his radio in and set it to the jazz station.

It was Virgil who'd thought somehow to give Jim a puzzle, once Jim was sitting upright in his bed. Virg had snuck in a small one of his own during one of our weekly visits, and when we weren't looking he put it on Jim's bed tray and turned the radio on. We turned around to see him spilling the pieces on the table, small pieces, two hundred as it said on the box. We thought that Jim might switch his grip to the tray and went to pack the puzzle up before he could spill it. Virgil sensed our motives and started his snorting and turned the radio up and blocked our path to the bed. I put a hand on his shoulder to move him, but the nurse stopped me. I looked up and saw Jim's steady hands working the pieces, lining the corners and sorting the colors. The puzzle box showed an oil painting of three pomegranates spilling their seeds onto a wooden table so that the seeds crowded one corner of the picture. Jim had the puzzle finished within two days, and upon doing so took to gripping at the sheets again. They had a small selection of hundred piece puzzles in the hospital's gift shop, and we bought every single one. I have to special order them in bulk from the catalogs now.

• •

Virgil had found this old toy radio in the basement one day when I'd left him unattended. Took him a while to figure out how to turn it on, on account of there being no batteries in it. He watched me put the batteries in and when he saw the metal contacts in the battery compartment his face grew and he started snorting and poking at the compartment and the leads. I pushed his hand away and he sniffed and teared up and so I let him have a close look at the compartment. Once he'd had his fill, I finished putting the batteries in and turned it on; Greensleeves spilled softly from the old speaker. I've gotten to know jazz well, because Virgil refused to listen to anything else. We had a few scares once he learned how to work the dial, and found himself lost in the static and broken up voices and country songs that crowd the radio around here. He'd panic and start snorting and twist the dial rapidly and shake it. Maybe he hoped he'd rattle the jazz onto the carpet.

After the accident our neighbor Harry brought us casseroles twice a week. He came in one evening when

Virgil had lost the jazz station and saw Virgil rolling on the floor and growling at the radio. Harry set the foil container on the counter and gave Charlie a quick pat on the head and went over to Virgil. He took the radio off the ground and Virgil sat up and watched close as Harry flipped through each station looking for a reaction. Virgil was nonresponsive until Harry found the jazz, at which point Virgil's eyes grew near twice their size. Harry knelt next to Virgil and brought the radio real close to Virgil's face, pointing at the station marking. Virgil's mouth hung wide open. Harry was silent for the entire interaction, and I didn't interject. Harry pulled a small pen and notepad from his back pocket and tore a few pages from the front before giving the pen and pad to Virg. Virg had been doing well in his writing lessons and could copy words just fine, but seemed to not know what they ever meant. Harry pointed at the dial and then at the paper and Virgil wrote the number down immediately. Then, keeping the radio right up next to Virgil's face, Harry moved the dial so the station was lost, and moved it back to the jazz. Virgil had started to drool a little, but watched on. Harry moved the dial again and handed the radio to Virgil, who in a moment snorted his panic off and cautiously turned the dial, watching the station marker until he found his station. Harry stood up and we both watched Virgil stand with the radio and stalk around the room, losing his station and finding it over again, turning his body with the dial and dancing around in the static.

Harry brought a small electrician's manual the next week. I told him Virgil couldn't read and he told me he couldn't either. He heard the jazz, Mingus, coming from Virgil's bedroom and knocked on the door. Virgil opened it and swiped the manual from Harry's hands and closed the door. Harry smirked at me and walked to his truck and returned with a spilling box full of old electronics and gadget magazines from when he was Virgil's age and set the box next to the bedroom door. Charlie pawed at the magazines until they spilled over the box's sides and settled into the box and fell asleep, purring. A light rain had started falling and Harry said he had to run on home before it worsened. I turned back to Virg's door and the box and cat were inside. I could see the box's shadow under the door.

• •

By the time Jim was as ready to come home as he ever would be, I made sure to set him up a place in the den. I found a card table and smaller coffee table in the basement and with Harry's help brought them upstairs. Rats had chewed through one of the coffee table's legs, and we fashioned a level for it out of a broken lampstand that we also found in the basement. We put the card table right in front of the fireplace, and set the coffee table next to it at a right angle. That way, it'd be easy to wheel Jim to the bathroom and couch where he would sleep. I had gone to Walmart and bought every puzzle they had using the first of Jim's disability and put them in the kitchen pantry.

We brought him home, him scanning out the windshield and gripping a tennis ball the entire time. I couldn't look at him much. I wasn't used to him sitting in the passenger seat.

I wheeled him up the yard, his eyes fixed on the telephone line the whole way. Harry had been waiting on the stoop the entire time and helped me lift Jim and his chair up the steps. We put him in front of the fireplace that Harry had lit and immediately spilled a five-hundred piece puzzle onto the table, setting the box on the mantle so Jim could see it. This one too was a painting; it showed a group of old-timers sitting on a riverbank, none looking at the other, only the river. Jim set to work immediately, and looked calm scanning and sorting the pieces, even though his eyes bulged. We placed a blanket over his legs to take the sharp heat from the fire and warm them. Virgil emerged from his bedroom with one of the new radios Harry had brought him from his workshop at home and carefully placed it on the table. According to the jockey, the next piece was an old Bill Evans tune. The music brought a calm into the room and then over Jim and Virgil. I went to the car and brought in my box of baby food. A typed out memo from the doctor was taped on top, listing Jim's feeding and, as the sheet put it, draining schedule. I dropped the box on the front step and sat down there.

• •

Virgil had picked up on the radios quick after Harry gave him the box of manuals. Soon enough the batteries in his first died and he learned how to open the back. Jim was working a puzzle in the den and Virgil was on the floor studying the radio. He started pulling out the transistors and wires and setting them each in a circle around him on the floor. Miles Davis trumpeted quietly from another radio brought by Harry. I asked about them and he said he was an enthusiast.

Satisfied that each part was accounted for on the carpet, Virgil began arranging them according to the old electrician's chart taken from Harry's box, checking the page carefully as he placed each wire. I went to him and offered to move him to kitchen table where he might have more room, but as soon as I started picking up his wires he started snorting and panicking so I set them back.

Harry saw them as they were the next day. He set down the casserole and went to Virg's door and tapped three times on it. Virg tapped back in time and Harry offered four more in swing as a return to which Virgil opened the door and followed Harry to the den. Harry sat Virgil on the floor next to the wires and put a hand on his shoulder and went outside to his truck. He came back with a piece of cardboard and a small box and sat opposite Virgil on the den floor. There was a cracking noise, and Jim was gripping onto the table and I went over and saw he had finished the puzzle. I quickly grabbed a tennis ball for him and pried his fingers around it, then slid the puzzle off the table and set it on the floor in the kitchen. I picked one from the pantry for him that showed a Norman Rockwell-style painting of a family sitting in a kitchen. A bright morning sun shone through the picture's windows. The family was each going about its routine: the father read his papers, the mother stirred oatmeal, and the child sat with a dog on the floor, which was black and white tile like our own kitchen's floor.

I took the puzzle to the den. Harry was laying out the contents of his box on the piece of cardboard, set between him and Virgil. Jim's head had started to loll back, and his eyes looked up toward the ceiling. I opened the box in front of him and spilled the pieces of the domestic scene onto the card table and set the picture on the mantle. I pulled the tennis ball from Jim's hand, and its grip fell to mine. He had done this in the hospital once and I cried, but the doctor told me it was an autonomic response. I said but what about the puzzles and he said the damaged mind attaches itself to certain functions sometimes. I said what about people and he said not likely.

I guided Jim's hand to the puzzle and as soon as he felt it, he tipped his head forward and set his eyes on it. I kissed him on his forehead which was cold. A light burning emerged behind me. I turned to Harry and Virgil, and Harry was melting a metal wire over the cardboard. Slowly, he had attached a wire to a small transistor, then another wire to the other side. He blew on the metal until there was no smoke and held it up for Virgil to inspect, then set it next to a schematic he had set next to the cardboard. When he handed the solder and iron to Virgil I told him best not let Virg handle it on account of him maybe hurting himself, but he said Virgil understood and I watched with no little apprehension as Virgil took his pudgy fingers to another wire and transistor and proceeded to melt the metal over them. Harry offered a quiet applause and I did too, and Virgil began to assemble the parts from the radio on his own. Harry brought in two more radios he'd brought from home. Within the month Virg had a full bookcase of radios Harry'd given him. Another month and he'd taken each apart and put them back together. He refused to work anywhere other than the den next to Jim, and every free surface, chair, couch, and sometimes Jim, was liable to be stuck with wires and melted with the iron. I'd tried to organize the parts for Virgil but he'd set to panicking soon as I would lay hands on them and spend hours rearranging them to his liking.

• •

Jim took to the jack-knife because I left it on the table for him. I was peeling an orange and Virgil had started whining over a dead wire sticking out of the carpet. I left the knife on the table without thinking and threw the orange peel into the fire-place which responded with a small burst. I saw to Virg, and before I realized it, Jim had stopped at his puzzle and was gripping the knife by its handle. I said Jim you'd best not hold onto that right now. I didn't expect him to respond or even hear me and he certainly did not. He sat there in his wheelchair with the knife in his right hand and a puzzle piece in the other. His eyes bulged as they always did; I could see the fire reflecting off of the blade and into his eyes which darted around the table and knife. I said 'Jim c'mon now,' but he still didn't respond. Virgil had yanked the wire from the carpet and took it and a few knobs scattered around the couch to his bedroom.

I stood there looking at Jim and him at the knife and puzzle piece. He brought the two close together and I thought he was going to cut himself but instead he gently took the knife to the piece and slowly whittled off the sides so that they were straight. He set the piece down and did the same with one after the other, forming a small pile of shaved cardboard on the table. I decided to stay next to him until he maybe gave up the knife or fell asleep.

After a few hours, watching Jim and listening to the quiet radio from Virg's bedroom lulled me to sleep. I don't remember all of what I dreamed, but I do recall at one point I was lying paralyzed from the neck down on the kitchen floor. Low cabinets lined the entirety of the room, in which there was no door. The cabinets were all closed but bright light shown through their edges. I called out for Jim but he didn't answer. I called out for Virg and felt him and turned my head to the side and saw him kneeling at the edge of the room, next to the cabinets. He looked older, not quite like Jim. His face was blank. He had his backpack on the ground next to him and without looking at it, reached in and began pulling out knobs of different sizes and shapes. I could hear a scratching coming from inside the cabinets. Seemed Virgil could too; he shuffled and hunched over along the cabinets with the pile of knobs cradled in his shirt. At each door he attached a knob at the center of it and carefully turned the knobs until he seemed satisfied. He went around the whole room, putting and setting a knob on each door. The scratching grew louder. Once he had outfitted every door, he crouched over to me and knelt above me. He was looking at one of the corners. I turned to look but I only saw darkness and the light from the cabinets. The scratching intensified more and steam started leaking from the light. Virgil had a single knob left and he pulled my shirt up just so my belly was showing and put the dial on it. I felt it merge with the skin but it wasn't painful. Virgil looked at me and spoke, but it was a language I couldn't understand. He looked me in the eye and I started to cry. He began to twist at the knob and I felt nothing but heard their scratching turn to squeals and saw that for every turn of the dial on my belly the cabinet doors began to open.

After a few turns I saw the first escape from its door and scamper toward me. I felt the second rat at my feet, which I noticed were bare. The rats had their teeth bared but their gazes were not angry, just blank like Virg's own stare. The first rat reached my arm and bit at my elbow. The other took to a toe, and more poured out of the cabinets. As soon as I saw blood flowing, a light formed in the ceiling, outlining a ragged square. I didn't feel any pain even as the rats covered and bit at every part of me. I felt drops of water on my head and saw the piece lift out of the ceiling to show the sky and the rain falling from the sky. I turned my head to escape the rain but a rat made for my eyes, so I turned to the sky again and let the rain blind me. The rain carried light with it. I looked at my body and the rats had chewed it down to the joints. Still I felt no pain. Virgil knelt to the side and the rats paid him no mind. I felt a shadow cast over me and the rain ceased and I looked up and two giant silhouettes emerged from the borders of the ceiling. They looked down at me and a light cast over their faces. I saw that they were me and Jim. Our faces were distant, seemingly unaware of the other. We opened our mouths and out poured a black pitch. The two streams of pitch merged and formed one and at the end of it a drop. As the drop grew so did the noises cease, the rain and the rats, until there was only a dull hum, and I felt my body dissolve under the rats until I was no longer a body and only my sight. The rats dispersed in lines back to the cabinets, and the drop filled my entire vision until there was no more and I shut my eyes to it, and with my eyes closed woke on the couch to the sight of Virgil kneeling over me.

His eyes were wide and he was breathing and sweating heavily and snorting. He held Charlie under an arm. I sat up on the couch and felt my body return and felt that the air had changed. Virgil was startled by my movement and sulked down onto the floor. I looked at the card table and Jim wasn't there. He and the chair had tipped over onto the floor and he was prone, gripping the knife and sawing at the carpet with it. The fire had gone out and only dim light shone from the kitchen. Virgil was looking around at Jim and the floor. Wires and dials and plastics were scattered around as always, but now in a different manner of disarray. The room was silent.

Virgil set his gaze finally on one of his radios, which lay face down on the floor in front of Jim. Its back was open; Virgil had probably meant to replace the batteries, but now all its wires were pulled out and torn. Jim still sawed at the carpet, eyes bulging and looking all around. I went to him and grabbed his wrist to get the knife away from him and saw his own arms and face were all cut up too. Even Virgil had some blood running down his fingers. I tried to get a grip on the knife handle, but Jim's was too strong and he started flailing the knife around and got me on my wrist. I put my whole weight on his arm which only seemed to strengthen his grip. My orange from earlier sat under the table and I grabbed it and set it in the blade's path. Juice squirted out when the blade went in, but I was able to work his fingers without fear of getting cut and finally got the knife out and threw it over into the kitchen. Jim's eyes dulled and he looked straight ahead at Virgil who watched quietly with the cat. Jim's hands went limp and he closed his eyes.

A pile of cardboard shavings had formed under the card table. The finished puzzle was laid out on it; the edges were square, but the picture was full of holes, its colors unmatched.

I caught my breath on the edge of the table, and Virgil

went around the room, inspecting the damage done. His gaze remained absent, and he let out an occasional snort regarding certain wires. He picked up the radio and turned the dial and no sound came out and he set it down again. He took a wire and prodded at Jim with it, then at Charlie, then stood up and sulked back to his room, carrying Charlie with him.

• •

Soon we could see the rain walling up against the other side of the hills, moving toward us fast. The telephone lines had now taken to a heavy sway. Once the rain hit us Virgil got real upset, and he switched his clawing to banging on the glass. I knew he was worried over the tree. Jim pulled him back but that only got him going worse, and he was big for being only ten, strong too, so he broke away from Jim without much struggle and kept running back to the door, Jim pulling him away in kind. Charlie heard the commotion and sat on the kitchen counter to watch. I took to holding Virgil back too, but as the rain grew so did his strength. We had both of us an arm finally and that seemed to subdue him for a time, but the real rain hit and sent the dogwood flowers across the yard, splattering against the window. The flowers pushed Virg further, and he started kicking and making that snorting noise he made when I think he meant to yell. The rain smeared the white flowers and pollen across the door, and through it we could see that the tree really was shaking, and Virgil just about as much. We had a hold of him though, until Charlie couldn't handle the excitement anymore and leapt from the counter to Jim and started clawing at Jim's neck and shoulders. Jim let go of Virg then, which left me with not much hold at all on his arm. He was reaching with all of him toward the door and the flowers and the tree, and I was tugging him back for all my own worth, but he wriggled free of my grip and sprung forward half running and rolling into the door, head and hands first. When the glass shattered with him there was a bang and a flash, and through the broken door I saw the fallen telephone pole and the line whipping back at the wind. Virgil wasn't slowed by the collision, and once he caught his feet he took off across the yard toward the tree, snorting and jumping at the blowing dogwood flowers as he went.

I turned to yell for Jim, but he was already running past me out the door and after Virgil, so I took off too. It was a choppy wind and the yard had already turned to mud and running was difficult for us, let alone bumbling Virg who by now was covered in mud and flowers and crawling still toward the tree. A telephone line whipped at the wind.

Virgil was about at the tree's base when Jim caught him and wrapped himself around him. I reached them both and pulled at them and we began toward the house, me pulling on an arm and Jim pushing and Virg wriggling and snorting. Halfway up the yard I lost my footing and fell, pulling Virg with me. Our fall sent Jim backward, and he caught himself on his knees. Virg was set to take off running again when the telephone line swung around and caught Jim on his bare arm, to which there was another bang and flash and Jim, kneeling, went stiff and the rain was silent and there was his silhouette kneeling in white light. All other shadows cast by the storm disappeared for that moment and Jim knelt in prayer to a self buried in mud.

• •

This is where he was when we buried it in the yard. I heard Charlie from the room and went to the door and heard Virgil snorting wild. No music came from any of his radios.

I asked the doctor and he said the mind is like wires, each a function, and that when those wires cross, sometimes things blur. I asked him about Charlie and he said for all Virg had decided, Charlie was no less a schematic than a radio. Than me or Jim.

I carried it in one of Harry's boxes to the tree. Virg was frozen on the steps. Jim slept on the floor in the den. Harry drove by and saw and sat in his truck but didn't leave it.

I think to myself now that there's no honor to be had in a funeral, that a life well-lived dies long before the body, or before a body even is. I see before me the mundane scenes of my own spent life and others, scattered pieces of a puzzle that's box is buried deep.

A small wind sent greens silent down the hills and field through the night and the tree shook. I shoveled out its loose soil with my hands, saying nothing.

• •

5 PIECES OF FLASH FICTION BY

Aaron Joel Lain
(Interpreting Chelsea Velaga)

1

Brenda held the door for her aging mother (who glided still, dying or not) and together they took a strange-but-not-that-strange pleasure in the astringency of the salon and the bright-pepto tiles that covered the floor and crawled up the walls and lit up the room like soft evening light. Brenda tilted her head toward her mother and whispered something, as if the tiles or plants were hiding microphones.

"I never thought I'd say it . . ."

"That you missed it?" her mother finished.

"Yeah."

"It's a sign of age and wisdom," her mother recited, "to come back home and realize it wasn't the devil you'd made it out to be."

Brenda, the long, Brenda the perhaps-too-thin, looked down and touched the long row of definitely-fake jungle plants that stood in the waiting area. Her skin bristled with vulnerability, a tingling, static-charge-feeling, and this in turn warped the world into something overwhelming; the passing moments buffeted her like hail. Her mother wouldn't say how sick she was, but the fact she said anything at all meant the outlook was grim.

The mother stooped (darkly draped in Hermès) and unclasped her black Louboutin's.

"These cost as much as a house in your country," she said to the little Cambodian woman whose dark eyes were as big as tea plates.

"We have so many new colors today," another, bossier Cambodian woman said, helping the mother into a puce-colored vinyl chair. The smell of acetone billowed around them.

Outside, the parking lot cooked in off-white sun and the air wavered like radiation. Beyond that, beyond the strip malls and a lonely, cracked highway stood the swamp, the trees themselves carnivorous and rising, dark as ferrofluid.

When it was Brenda's turn to pick a color, she erred on the side of blue.

• •

2

Rachel can't contain herself. She squirms in the backseat. We tell her to be cool, that once we pick up a few things we will head to the party. She plays with the vinyl seat cover that's peeling off. Rachel talks about the last party, how many shots she did, how many boys she kissed. She puts her hand over her eyes, feigning embarrassment, but the pallor of her voice is bright and self-assured—she loved it, and she wants us to know it without having to be too obvious. We run a red light. The cops have long since abandoned this place. Rachel's voice grows fainter and fainter from the backseat of the car. We pull over and assess the situation. How could we have missed it? What we thought was Rachel, the corporeal, flesh-and-organ-girl was a manifestation of something—like a shared memory, a projection or hologram of our collective longing. We remember that Rachel was last seen at a supermarket in the town over, lining up boxes of cake mix, wearing a red apron around her waist. She stood in the aisle and admired her work, the beauty-as-precision, the cathartic neatness. There was a heavy rainfall outside and through the gray-blue haze of falling water, she saw a figure emerge from a pickup truck. His arms were outstretched like Christ, and behind him was a child floating like a balloon. The man reached into the rain, his face tilted to precipitous heaven, and he caught the child and brought him back down. She thought she could see his face. She thought his name was David.

3

"There is victory in Jesus," a small radio says. It sits in the window. Every three months someone comes along and replaces the batteries. Over the years, it's grown a heathy bed of flowers in its tape-deck and lush grass in its speakers. Then the radio went silent.

A woman glances at herself in the mirror and sees her mother's body. We decay differently, we decay the same, she says. Her husband barges in with the broken radio. He takes it apart, laying the pieces in precise, modular lines on the slate-blue carpet. Rich soil clumps between the pieces.

Don't step on him, he says to his wife. Don't step on our son.

Snowfall in Arizona. The desert is painted ironoxide

beneath the fluorescent-white blanket of snow. The red comes through in bloody patches.

They had a dog once, a little white dog, whose breath became atrocious as he aged. He'd made love to nearly every pillow in the house. A picture on the fridge shows the woman, the man, the radio, and the tip of whoever's finger was taking the picture. The dog is somewhere out of frame, giving it to a stranger's rolled-up beach towel.

When the man has taken apart the radio, he listens to the circuit boards for a heartbeat. There's a twinge of pain in his head, just behind his left eye. I can hear it, oh I can hear it, the man says, tears flowing down his face. His wife continues her self-inspection in the mirror as water begins to steadily drip, drip, drip from the light fixtures, forming dark continents in the carpet. Someone once said to her: you can't go back and do things over, and they were right. Maybe she will convince her husband to buy her another dog.

The water is cold, but baby we're colder.

• •

4

Walgreens, Gallatin Pike

I was stooped by the epsom salt and in enormous pain. You leaned against the candy aisle and made faces in the band of mirrors along the back of the store. I was certain you could hear me complain and curse. When I turned to look at you, I saw my husband again, just as he was forty years ago. Still in those high-waisted corduroys and round glasses. As I stood up I felt my own body begin to change. I felt my back straighten, my bones thickened like demi glacé, my breasts re-inflated. So much pain, gone, boiled away. Everything was bright again, like snow in the sun. I turned to you and asked where I'd seen you before. Around, you said. My new-again thighs quivered at the sound of your voice.

• •

5

Five days after losing his job he was still on the couch. He hadn't changed clothes or bathed since and his unkempt, wiry beard bore a faded orange dusting of nacho flavor. She'd had enough; she was sick of him watching daytime courtroom shows and filling the house with farts. She pulled him up and made him shower. Then she took him to the park where the two of them walked the bike trails which were mostly empty. She held his hand and pointed out the different birds (she didn't know their names, but that didn't stop her from saying whatever bird-name-sounding thing popped into her head as she saw them bathing in dust or flitting through the brush or singing from the half-shadows of baby trees).

He was ambivalent.

They turned and walked down a nature trail. On their right stood a curtain of honeysuckle bristling with phallic pre-blooms (white and green) and the smell was intoxicating. She took his hand and plucked one of the blooms and he held his hand open and looked at the bloom for a long time. The warmth of the sun and the cool breath of the wind did something to him. They went back home and got drunk.

Long ago they'd decided to abandon fear, to be more open with one another. There's no vulnerability like being tied up or chained, being completely helpless to the whims of someone, even someone you think you know.

At any time, he thought, she could put her hands around my neck and squeeze until my eyes popped out. Sometimes she did that very thing as she rode him, often to the point where his peripheral vision became blurred and brown and he felt as if he were sinking out of his body.

But she always knew when to stop.

She welcomed him back to the world of the living with her body, the warmth and wet and her voice (muffled by dark latex) calling him a cum-filled, shit-stained whore. He was resurrected, born again, new. She was his salvation, his mercy, his nirvana.

He was her pet, her toilet, her baby, her entire heart.

• •

PERSPECTIVE
BY

Moriah Claud
(Interpreting Michelle Farro)

Perspective

I'm looking
from the outside
now. The walls
look the same
from here. Your
Paradise,
I lost it.
paradis perdus
You didn't make me leave
but I didn't want to stay
I took the apple with me when I left
piece together my features
the curve of your nose
the color of his eyes in the sun
but I'm not on the mantel
in your wedding dress
paradis retrouvé
(you are beautiful even when I don't want you to be)
now that we have it, what do we do?

5 SELECTED POEMS BY

Robyn Leigh Lear
(Interpreting Olivia Keaggy)

stroked within a world of breezed dances trying to
control a blend
salt mixed with cadmium
black becomes crystallized
grey becomes iris
(eyes a black pit)
She stands unafraid.

textured inside a dark cave as the earth breathes
fluidity into the paint
salt mixed with indigo
two are combined forever in a suspended
beautiful lifeless blush
"eyes to heaven
eyes to hell"
She stands unafraid.

oceans of magnesium thrust against rusted gated
collapsed canvas
salt mixes in blank pages
the ink dries as paint breathes
he touches her
she touches her
(without hands—only in limited art forms)
as shadows pass through strands
limitless potential
She stands unafraid

Creat[ive] Fear: Pen, Brush, Chord, and Consciousness

"I was teased by your [perspectives]
Spit out by your mouth
I was loud by your lowered
Seminary soul"

cold in the kind of way where your teeth chatter
rhythmic sensation that correlates to the celestial
stirrings of the sun setting on snow

Warm in a way that leaves the tips of fingers still
cooling between the breaths after love making is
finished and the noon sun erases your shadow in
the mint field highlighting curved connection...

Heat. Hot. Heavy is the dissipating microscopic
tether binding the mind to shore as it mixes with
earth in a penetrating release.

I was captivated by your blossoms
Consumed by your beast
I screamed in the silence
Of your seminary soul

Ekphrastic poem inspired by: Olivia Keaggy
and Bon Iver's "Creature Fear"

To An Aesthete Who Likes To Watch

Considering the act of creation as an act of found colors—
they bend and breathe in spaces where stellar
caresses bend wood to brush. As the color dries,
shines, and grows and inside dark crevasses ringing
like a tantalizing cry for the New direction—lost.
Screams silenced in the
reeling
rebellion against the formless
only to be met
with broken language
yelling into the shapeless

We are the mad mundane. Wailing profanities in squalor
lamentations where the sunrises, shines, and falls into duller
shapes and shades: fluid, untouched by blind false notion
holding the hand of
grey scales of truth
bibulous forbidden daydreams
intended fucks
vigorous
vitality

The unforeseen consequence of the sunset is the fading, duller,
fevered colors with red reds and violent violets;
cascading into calmer, cooler
continuations recycled like another dying day
concluding with silent color
voiced by artists singing. The seer is the glossy-eyed fractured mirror
reminding us meaningful memories why:

"you are the beauty you wish, the sound you hear, the truth you color"

• •

To A Bibliophile Between the Sheets

A poem sounds like eyelashes
smashing against mocking bird wings
feathering lies
calling out questions
unbound

A poem feels like a lightning storm
flashing against the clouds
crashing into a cell tower
canceling sound
broken

A poem looks like oceans lakes sand soil nurtured
on abstractions
looking to understand the sensual contact of hands
circulation between oxygen and grey smoke
exploding heat and perfume
questions.

A poem smells like moon flowers and honeysuckles
becoming a sensational act reading
fluttering toward intangible
wandering between the desert and ocean
daydreams

A poem tastes like honey as it coats the tongue with crystals
culminating into a lonely isolation
living in words that do not *fit what they are trying to say*
refreshing and bitter like lemons
unknown

• •

Damned Scribbling

A fascination between the curves in a blank
Vibrant visualizations as lightning storms rule
The vantage points. The curves bend break
underneath
          The weight of the
                    Clouds covering
                              Memories
                              Moonflowers
                              Cherry blossoms
                              Golden rain
                              Brushed hair

A formation develops around curvature
The forested imagination discovering a world out
Side its trees. I feel chrysanthemums cry
          From beneath the significance
                    The ground covers
                              Isolation
                              Memories of wet prose
                              Deep creased folds
                              Iridescent inkwells.

A fumbling for light happens when the darkness
Haunts the spaces between you and the light
Where the wreckage becomes stronger than a
Second chance
To dance in lightning
Cracks
Crashes
Calls
Candesces

A foundation lays out a structured wall
Where the windows open, night flowers, breeze blows
Through and throughout. Rustling pages
Pretty lights
Cascading sun
Shining pen
Crisp page
To dance in lightning
Beneath the insignificance
The vantage point of the female pen—I imagine.

THIS BOY, THIS CITY, THIS HOLY OBJECT A STORY FOR CHILDREN BY

Barry Kitterman
(Interpreting Tim Durham)

On his seventh birthday Otto woke up, petted the cat once, the dog twice, peed in the toilet (he thought about peeing in the sink but he didn't) and stood on the edge of the bathtub so he could see if he had grown overnight. He decided he had, though he knew it was easy to make a mistake along those lines. He also knew this day was going to be a day like no other day in the entire history of Otto. Today would mark the beginning of the new Otto. From now on, everyone would say, I remember the old Otto. He was nice enough.

Downstairs, the woman who lived at his house was preparing the morning meal. Otto watched her go about her tasks, the woman who until this day had been known by a name of her own, but who forever after would be known simply as Otto's mother.

"Otto," said the woman. "Your name is on backwards."

Otto took a deep breath and reached for the sharp knife he carried in his waistband at all times, only to find it wasn't there.

"I think I'll start carrying a knife," he said, and the woman nodded her silent agreement.

"I think you should," she said, keeping silent no longer. "Things need to be sawed and hacked and shredded."

"Sometimes I have to defend myself," said Otto.

"I don't doubt it," said the woman.

Otto wondered what small animals she had slaughtered for his breakfast. He watched as she poured a heavy bowl full of grains from the field and placed a small amount of the milk from a wild cow in the same bowl.

"Did you sleep well, my lord?" she asked.

"Well enough," said Otto. And when she turned her back to do more of the women's work that her kind were in the habit of doing, he took the knife from the butter dish, wiped it clean on the leg of his pants and tucked it into his waist. It was cold against his skin.

Cold steel. He imagined saying it out loud, but knew things had gone too far for that.

"I expect you'll be home for dinner," said the woman.

He slipped out the door. There was a world outside.

In the vast expanse that surrounded the dwelling he

shared with the woman (and the man who claimed to be her own), Otto breathed in the morning air. He could hear far away noises from the neighboring estates, but he focused on the world before him. It was dangerous to do anything else. The grass at his feet looked as if it had grown a foot overnight. He would speak to the peasants. The place needed a reasonable buffer, a safe zone between the building where he slept and the silent expanse of trees and ravines and rockslides and sinkholes he knew to be out there beyond the safe haven. Men went into that forest and didn't return.

"It's because they aren't prepared," he said to his right hand man, who stepped forward from the shadows. "The shadows of memory," whispered Otto. And then, "You're here."

When the man didn't respond, Otto looked him up and down for any signs of treachery. Finding none, he showed his right hand man the blade he always carried in his waistband.

"This will protect us," said Otto.

"My lord," said the man from the shadows of memory.

"Stand over here," said Otto. "On my right hand side."

The man touched his fist to his forehead and moved as Otto told him.

"Drop down and give me fifty," whispered Otto.

As they prepared for their departure, Otto rankled at the man's many questions.

"I may have forgotten your name," said Otto.

"I am Hugo, my lord. I keep the memory."

"Don't fail me, Hugo."

"What are we searching for? The way is dangerous. The roads are lined with silent trees that watch and wait for any misstep."

"Is your courage that of a man, or a boy?" asked Otto.

"Let us bring the dogs at least," said the man called Hugo.

"If they choose to come. If not, we go anyway."

"Let us bring the horses," said Hugo. "At least the horses."

"Horses," said Otto. "I don't need horses."

"My lord," said the man yclept Hugo.

And on the second day of their journey they realized they were thirsty. "Is there water?" asked Hugo.

The man's weakness was a trial to Otto. Hugo's long hair, falling across his face, his fearful mien, all of these gave Otto pause.

"Have courage," said Otto. "I have gone days without water. I have gone years without food."

"I follow you," said Hugo, his eyes dark with respect.

"Often," said Otto, "when you are in need, the great world will provide."

"I believe in your leadership," said Hugo.

A long snake lay uncoiled in the tall grass, its sides green and shiny, thin filaments of gold spiraling into the distance.

"This snake will give us water," said Otto.

"Kill it first," whispered the vassal Hugo.

Otto took the knife he kept with him always in his waistband, and threw it in a perfect arc. It landed on the flat end, yet it stunned the snake, hitting the beast in the testicles, and Otto leapt into action, pulling the snake's belly to him and severing it, leaping back to watch the snake writhe in mortal farewell.

"Drink," he said to Hugo. Otto always let his men drink first. "Drink, and then I will drink."

"You are good," said Hugo.

Otto returned the blade to his waistband. He drank the blood of the snake. It refreshed him.

"Are you replenished?" he asked Hugo.

"I am, my lord."

"Watch vigilantly while I relieve myself against this foul tree," said Otto.

"I see a harpy in the distance. She would speak."

"I have no time for harpies," said Otto. "I am doing a man's work here."

"I will ignore her on your behalf, my lord."

"As you should," said Otto.

They journeyed on for many days. At times they knew they were risking their lives. More than once, Otto had to rescue Hugo from danger.

One day a wild animal that looked like the forest itself came to the edge of the clearing where they had spent the night under the stars and the three moons of the realm. The animal had a fierce look in its eye, and it clearly was famished. It had not eaten for a time beyond measuring, and it looked hungrily at Hugo, not caring if Hugo wore his hair over one eye and carried a magic backpack with all the things his lord needed. To the animal, Hugo looked like a much-needed meal.

"No," said Otto.

He held his hand out. The beast could feel the energy Otto sent forth from his open palm.

"Don't eat Hugo. Instead, come and be one of us."

"I will," said the animal, surprising Otto with his ability to speak, but only a little. Otto had seen this kind of thing before, in the years gone by.

"Do you know any magic?" Otto asked the beast. "For I know a lot of magic, but there may be some magic I don't know that you could teach me which might come in handy in facing danger in the future. There's a lot of danger."

"I know how to blend into the forest," said the creature.

"I have seen you do that," said Otto. "I believe you speak

truth."

"My lord," said the creature.

"Do you have a name, friend?" said Otto.

Faithful Hugo came to stand at Otto's side. Hugo had a blade, too, although his was smaller than Otto's blade and not as sharp.

"This thing that stands before us," said Hugo. "Is it safe?"

"We needn't worry," said Otto. "There's room for him in this world. There's a task for him."

"They call me William," said the beast. "For I am noble."

Otto placed his hand on Noble William's head.

"I must go relieve myself," said Noble William.

"That's understandable," said Otto. "It's fit that we relieve ourselves. Whenever we need to."

Hugo was already relieving himself, giving little regard for the danger of it. High above, a bird the size of a small town dove in Hugo's direction.

"Mr. Hugo," shouted Noble William, and he threw himself forward to take the blow of the bird's wrath, but Otto too saw the danger, and needed only to take the blade from his waistband and let it catch the light of the midday sun, and the bird went shrieking away into the sky.

"You're good with that thing," said Noble William.

"I owe you my life," said Hugo, brushing the hair away from his gaunt face. "I fear it is the hunger that made me lose my focus."

"We are all hungry," said Otto. "Hunger is only one of our enemies."

"My lord," said Hugo, cinching his belt tighter, donning a look of renewed determination.

"I must ask," said Noble William. "What is our task?"

Otto stood very still. He lifted a finger to determine which way the wind was blowing. He smelled the wretched pottage coming from the campfires of the people native to these strange parts. He wondered if it would be safe to approach them and ask for sustenance.

"A city lies deep in these woods, one that has been forgotten for many centuries," said Otto.

"I know the one," said Noble William.

"May I call you Bill?" asked Hugo.

"I don't think so," said Noble William.

Otto signaled to Hugo that he should hold his peace and respect the ways of the forest.

"I will lead you to the city," said Noble William.

On the dawn of a new day, they came to an enemy camp, tents in the clearing. They decided they would carry out a raid, not trusting the false words spoken by the harpy who guarded the enemy's horde of food. Hugo offered to go into the camp of their foe, but Otto knew that sometimes a commander in chief had to do a thing. He would not ask one of his men to do anything he wasn't willing to do himself, take any risk, run through a gauntlet and remain unscathed.

"I will get us something to eat," said Otto. He ordered Hugo to pull the hair back away from his eyes.

"How do you see where you're going?" he said

"It would be wise to act now," said Noble William. "While the harpy is distracted."

Otto pried open the door to the harpy lair, silently. He reached out to the blade he carried in his waistband and found reassurance there.

The harpy had set out food on a rough table, as if she were preparing to feed her own brood. He wondered for a moment if he would be robbing from the mouths of harpy babes. Perhaps this was why they were so dangerous. Had they been mistreated by the race of men?

He would just take what he needed. Bread and meat, cheese from the milk of cows or whatever foul beasts the harpy controlled. There was a hard substance, some kind of plant from the looks of things. He would leave it for the harpy children.

"Come," he commanded his companions, and they ran safely into the woods where they shared the food.

"You take most of it," said Noble William. "You need the strength to guide us."

"I rely on you," said Otto. "You must take us to the city."

"Is there enough for me?" asked Hugo.

"Of course," said Otto. "There's enough for all."

"I have the strength to go on," said Noble William.

"Does anyone need to relieve himself?" asked Otto.

"I'm good," said Hugo.

In the 26th month of that year, they stood on a hill and looked at the city before them. The city was a cruel city, and cruel people lived there, although only the leaders of the city were cruel. The people were victims of the leaders. It was always this way, thought Otto. People had looked to him for help before.

"What shall we do?" asked Hugo. "Should we take out our blades and charge through the city gates, freeing the oppressed, setting fire to the stockpiles of weapons? Or should we meet in the middle of the road and tell them we mean business?"

"We could slip through the back way," said William. "There's a tunnel and a river and a boat."

"I will consider all of these fine plans," said Otto. "I would like to minimize the loss of life at a time like this."

"My lord," said Hugo.

Otto was pleased to see that Hugo no longer wore his hair over his face.

"You can see better this way," said Otto.

"I can," said Hugo. "I will never doubt you again."

"Your doubts do you honor," said Otto. "I want no lackeys."

Suddenly they were surrounded by a pack of fierce jungle beasts, snarling and glowering and swearing in their own language. Otto wondered if he would be able to reason with these. He tried to speak to them in English, and then in Spanish. He spoke to them in the universal language of men.

"They continue to snarl and swear," said Hugo.

"Do you know sign language?" said Otto.

"I do," said Noble William.

William, the noble one, made several wise gestures asking for peace.

"They say they are going to kill us and eat us."

"Are they very hungry?" asked Otto.

William made several more gestures.

"They say they have no respect for the law. I fear they are just bad."

"They're like zombies," said Hugo. "Remember when we met the zombies?"

"A lifetime ago," said Otto.

He took hold of his blade, glad that he always carried it in the waistband of his tunic.

"This tunic can repel many things. But I worry about these forest beasts. Their eyes are angry and red."

"Tell us what you want us to do," said Noble William.

Otto surveyed the foe that had gathered. Thousands of them. Some rode on horseback and others drove complicated engines of war unlike anything Otto had ever seen, although he was sure he could drive one. Sadly, he turned to his companions.

"Sometimes, it's nothing to do but fight," he said.

"My lord," said Hugo.

"We fight then," said Noble William.

The battle went on for days. Each time Otto thought he had dealt with the worst that the beasts had to offer, each time he thought they had turned and faded away into the trees, another wave attacked from a new angle. He had never realized the world had so many angles. Twice he had to save Noble William, and at least five times he stood in front of Hugo and took the blows of the enemy with his tunic. Without his help, Hugo would not have made it through the battle.

Finally, just one frightening, very bad beast remained to be dealt with. It was Noble William who urged Otto to step back and let him fight this last opponent.

"You're tired," said William.

"I am wounded," said Otto.

"It's just a flesh wound," said Hugo. The hair had fallen across his worried brow.

But before Otto could speak, Noble William threw

himself into the fray. He fought like two Williams, and the other beast fought like twenty beasts. They fought in the dirt, they fought in the trees, they grew wings and flew through the sky. Hugo wanted to jump in and help the Noble William defeat the horrible beast, but Otto stayed Hugo's arm.

"It would break William's heart," said Otto. "You must let William reach the end of his own fate, whatever may come. It is the way of all his kind."

William fought with courage, but being truly noble, he was having a hard time killing the beast. He held the stunned beast by the throat and looked to Otto.

"What is your wish, my lord?"

In the moment of hesitation that comes over the best of heroes, William's fate was in play. The evil beast threw dirt in Noble William's eyes, and then the beast (who had no name) sprang up and sliced Noble William's head clean off his shoulders. The head settled back exactly in place, and for a moment Otto was able to talk to William.

"Thank you, my friend, for protecting me on this journey."

William tried to speak, but it was hard.

Hugo wept.

And then Otto felt the dark rage of justice wash over him. He took the blade from his waistband, and feinted to the left, then swirled the blade in the light of the sun, blinding the beast who would have killed them all.

"You have left me no choice," said Otto, and he stabbed the beast forty times in the heart.

Otto was wounded severely in the epic battle, and it was up to Hugo to bind Otto's wounds.

"I thought the tunic would save you," said Hugo.

"I thought so too," said Otto.

"Will you live?"

"My wounds are nothing."

And Hugo wept some more.

They approached the city on horseback. (The horses had walked up to them in the clearing and knelt so that Otto and Hugo could climb on their backs.)

"We will take you to the city," said the horse that offered his back to Otto. "You will find it much to your liking."

"I thought it was an evil place," said Hugo.

"No," said the second horse.

"I admire the way you talk," said Hugo. "You hardly have any accent."

"We studied hard," said the horse, "in school."

"Tell me of the city," said Otto. "My wounds make me weak. And the day is dying."

"It is a place of beauty," said the first horse. "Men and horses live here in peace. The harpies take care of all our needs."

"Hugo," said Otto, "come and ride close by my side and hold me up on the back of this horse. I grow weary. I grow weak. It has been a long time since we found food."

"Do you need to relieve yourself?" whispered Hugo.

"I'm fine," said Otto.

"We have doctors in the city," said the second horse. "The people await you. The horses sing your praises. You slew the beasts we were afraid of."

"The beasts," murmured Otto.

"My lord," whispered Hugo.

"I feel faint," said Otto.

When he awoke, he was surrounded by smiling people. Some of them were old and wrinkled, and those had been harpies when they were enchanted by the evil beasts. Some of them were young and had never known the evil of the world.

"Where is my blade?" said Otto, for he had grown accustomed to its presence in his waistband.

"You don't need it here," said the horse he had rode in on. The horse was mostly white with large black patches.

"You're a pinto," said Otto.

The gentle horse had tears in his eyes, grateful that Otto had recognized him for all that he stood for.

"The people have something they want to give you," said the pinto.

Three small children appeared, as if they hadn't even been there a minute before. They carried an object made of gold, filled with wonder, the thing Otto knew he had been looking for all this time.

"It's a morpolax," said the oldest of the children. "It's yours." Otto knew, though they were the children of the harpies, they would never grow up to be harpies themselves.

"Take it with you," said the harpy child. "Keep it safe."

"My lord," whispered Hugo.

"I will do as the children say," said Otto.

He turned to face the assembly, which had grown in large numbers. They all bowed and made the sacred symbol, putting their fists to their foreheads, then tapping their fists twice on the earth. Once for respect and a second time for respect too.

"From this day forth," said Otto, "I will keep this sacred trust. I will never forget you. Teach the children of your children that there is always a good way to live. And remember, if ever you need me again ..."

His words couldn't be heard for the mighty roar that went up from the crowd. All the people and all the horses knew what he was going to say, and they approved.

"Come Hugo," said Otto. "It's time we went home."

"My lord," said Hugo.

The horses took them as far as the edge of the meadow.

WITH GUN, 6 MAY 2016

BY

Ericka Suhl
(Interpreting Savannah Weaver)

At 8:30 a.m., the girl was still missing. An amber alert had flashed on my phone the day before. The feeling of urgency and helplessness had not diminished through dinner, baths, sleep, or breakfast. While driving my son to school, leaving the house at 8:20, the news over the radio provided more details. She was released from school to an uncle. He had come for her, worried about the girl's father who had been in an accident. The school let her go, but there was no accident. I had little hope that she would be found alive. We are all still looking for a little girl with long, blond hair, blue eyes, and the mixture of baby and permanent teeth that all nine-year-olds show off when they smile.

By 9:05 a.m., everything was packed and ready to go. The weather was cool and sunny, and all the blossoming trees had run through their flowerings into fat leafiness. The only thing that felt wrong was a slight change in the way I wore my backpack because of my gun. My purple holster pushed the gun up into my backpack's waist straps, and I couldn't set as much weight from the pack on my hips. The gun carried a loaded magazine, but there was no bullet in the chamber. I was too afraid of some unimaginable thing accidentally pulling the trigger back and firing the gun into my leg. I practiced walking around my bedroom with the gun hidden inside the waistline of my pants, and the barrel end that peeked out of the holster pressed into the top of my thigh with each step. I resolved to remain soldier straight through the hike, like a Tin Man who could not fold. It took more than one trip to load my gear in the car because I took the gun separately and hid it in the console.

There were only 5 cars in the park at around 9:25 a.m., and I was troubled that there were so few people there. I looked over to where Jill normally parked when we met there to hike the trails together. We had been practicing for a big 130-mile hike until she twisted her ankle while climbing a hill, reciting poetry at the same time. Jill hates guns, and I had become used to hiking without it for her sake. For my sake, she assured me that her 6 ft stature would ward off anyone who would do me harm. Without her, alone, I took the gun out of the console and stuffed it down my pants until the clip snapped in place over my belt. I slipped an extra magazine of .380 rounds into my pocket. With my shirt hanging loosely over it, I imagined it looked like nothing anyone should worry about, but the bulge from the gun stood out, like a growth on my hip, as soon as I fastened my backpack into place. I felt too much weight on my back instead of my hips, but with the gun bobbing up into my waist with every step, there was no help for it.

I started my runner's watch with its built-in GPS once I hit the shade of the tree-lined entrance to the park. Surely there was a way to hack into such things if they needed to find me and if every second counted. I approached the ruined dance and bandstand area that led to a cave, a cave that ran into the heart of the park. It was the convergence spot for all the trails, and a man was standing where couples used to spend Friday nights cheek to cheek listening to big band music. He was white, 5' 10", and approximately 200 lbs with a bald head surrounded by blond stubble. His back was to me as he read a stand of commemorative plaques that had been placed in the middle of the dance floor. At 9:30 a.m., I walked quickly down the steps that led to a path that would take me under the dance floor and close to the cave entrance. The clicks of my hiking poles echoed into the cave, and I was so preoccupied with the man on the level above me that I failed to pay attention to the shadows around the cave to see if they were moving. I picked the lakeside trail and walked back out into the sunlight, and possibly because of the man's visibility, braced for something to come down upon me. I only looked back a couple of times because there is a game to be played. One must act normal. Carrying the gun did not make me feel better.

The point at which the trail turned up into the forest was harder to find due to the thicker foliage. The leaves were back, so the shadows were also back. The approach into the forest was steep, and my new poles were put to the test. I was clumsy with them, not as sure as I usually felt using a pole I had found in the snow fields of Mt. Rainier. I first used it to get from Camp Muir at 10,000 ft back down to the Paradise parking lot. A lot of things are forgotten and left behind on that hike, and due to some miscommunication among my climbing mates, I had been forgotten too. The sunset drew lines of gold light and mountain shadow into itself until there was nothing left. I want to tell you all about the spur I found myself on, thrust out above the whole green world of the Cascades, and how alone, yet peaceful, I felt there in the dying purple light, but it was dark. I finished the hike with my headlamp on, stopping every fifty or so steps to look behind me. Female forest rangers had been lured away and assaulted repeatedly on the Skyline Trail. It was not safe. It was during one of those turns that my headlamp lit up a young man wearing a hoodie, white, 5' 8" and approximately 150 lbs. I screamed loudly in his face. He hadn't made a sound behind me. He made the mistake of asking me questions, trying to become familiar, because it is the people who are familiar that do the most damage. I couldn't act normal anymore, and I ran the rest of the way to the parking lot. It was illegal then to carry a gun in a National Park, but I had my pole.

Jill insisted that I try to find better, lighter poles that were properly sized. They were working out well at 9:35

a.m., but it was hard to notice because I was still worried about the man at the bandstand, and what he would do next. At the crest of the ridge, I saw a man standing next to a tree by the trail. My already sick heart beat faster. I dug the poles firmly into the soft earth ahead of me, hoping I'd be able to pull the slide back and chamber a round into my gun without shaking so badly that the gun would be useless. The white male, 220 lbs., 6', was holding one of three little dogs, and his hiking partner, a woman, came huffing and puffing up the opposite side of the ridge just as I arrived near the top. I relaxed just a little, glad that someone was at the park besides the man reading about the history of the dance floor. We all bid each other a good morning.

The other side of the ridge was darker and cut deeper into the earth. There were cold areas where the cave running under the park slowly exhaled. Something was going wrong with my vision when I saw a little girl skip down one of the boardwalks, coming toward me. She was alone, and I noticed right away that her hair was blond. Just as I was wondering why that seemed familiar to me, her family, all women, swayed into view as if from a mist. They moved like slow giants around her rapid little heartbeat pounding skips on the boardwalk. I watched her until one of my poles got stuck between the slates of the bridge, and while I, embarrassed, struggled to wrench it free, they all disappeared down the trail together. I looked forward again and another woman floated toward me with a camera that had a long, zooming eye. Her center of gravity swung way, way up into the leafy tree tops, into the wind, and she looked down for a moment at me to say good morning.

Next to their lightness, I felt heavy in my arms and shoulders, knees and ankles. My movements clanged and banged together like I was made of stock pots and toaster ovens. I stabbed my poles in regular time with my heavy breathing and worked up each ridge, stopping for no reason at all. Only a few things stood out to me, like one, lone leaf that had fallen into a rare ray of sunlight in the lowest part of the forest. The leaf glowed like a firefly, and I could see the machinery with which it turned light into nourishment. I glanced at it for just a moment, like passing a handsome man whom I should not be caught gazing at. In the distance, a small woman came from around a bend in the trail, and I recognized her from hikes with Jill. She was a regular at the park, and most noted for carrying some kind of hidden radio with her. As I passed her and said, "Hello," I could hear Korean music magically emanating from her belly. I imagined that she had left a trail of her music behind her, making safe the half of the loop I had yet to finish. I stopped, took off my pack to get my water, and stood up without the weight of it on my back. Intending to put the cold bottle to my forehead, I bumped my sunglasses that had been on the whole time.

At 10:00 a.m. I took off my sunglasses. Gold light poured into the forest and lit up the trail ahead of me. Determined to become more comfortable, I adjusted my gun, played with the straps on my pack, and set off again with my poles making light "pat, pat" sounds like soft, little bells. The trail rolled smoothly over roots and rocks and in and out of shadow, and I rolled smoothly along with it. My body enjoyed the desire to move forward, taking the turns with efficiency and ease. Even the gun seemed to melt, soften and sleep against my hip. It moved benignly with my movements instead of bouncing awkwardly. I spent the rest of the hike stopping to take in sounds that did not fill me with fear. If I kept walking, I could have stayed in that state beyond the membrane of fear a little longer, or at least until the man from the dance floor appeared around that corner. Or this corner. Or the next. But it was a good morning, and I finished my work early that day. At 2:09 p.m., my husband responded to my text about maybe getting something to eat or some coffee: "Yeah. Wherever you want to go."

It was 3:30 p.m. when the voice on the radio said that several people had been shot in Maryland. I drove to my son's school to pick him up again, and learned that the shooter had murdered his estranged wife in the parking lot of a high school. The console in my car was empty because I had unloaded my gun and put it away after the hike. I felt how empty it was.

• •

5 POEMS BY

Austin Boling
(Interpreting Seth Prestwood)

ON ALL THE HAPPY MORNINGS

life is very easy when the trees are caked in
orange I stare out the window
bit-lipped in the kitchen's brightness
I try to compare things to
other things cherry pittings &
paint fumes I cuss & I cuss & I hear
myself cuss my body prays this way
concrete-scabbed all dangle-faced &
grab-fucking something to be hidden

• •

A POEM ABOUT PHRENOLOGY

here's a certainty   it is good to be sad & say
nothing   to unhinge a bone

from a shoulder socket   from your mouth

            cushioned with soft taffy   to press

underneath your tongue   with your tongue

            rounding & splotched   to be torn

                        I want to show you something

            in my head   everything is always happening

I take up space   I say a marsh of words

I pull the bees out of my mouth

                                        & the world goes blank

AUBADE

in morning light   gurgling over a low flame
I have several feelings   about the hunk of
beef in the fridge   the sprigs of onion &
pepper flakes   the cilantro plants   freshly
potted   or my body's strange sounds   I think
of how everything sounds like air   as I walk
        from one end of the room   to the other
& the choke-collared dog pants its music
        still spinning slightly   I crack an egg
                & try to cut lemons with my teeth

I AM ONLY ONE PART OF THE RABBLE

pressing dollar bills into my palm notes of oak
& tinged-leather or sweat drenched
in the alabama pines
I chew-&-chew-&-chew-&-chew
I salt-pepper blossom
blossom-crowned skull pock-marked
& spilled coffee
stains the rim of my mug
coneflowering I think of your little buddha
to fill the half-day with blue

WHEN I AM HOPELESSLY OPTIMISTIC

I am in the room   with the beer cans again
I walk from that room   to another room
            slick-pitted   sugar-fevered
winter arrives   in my head only
each dull thud of falling apples   or the
sink stained from a week   of pouring
coffee grounds   over the dishes   milk &
pink
my eyes cull shapes   on the black lawn
dark poplars   carp head
I sleep on my stomach   & drift though
            I am up to my wrists in blind spots

IT MAY MANY

BY

Matt Johnstone
(Interpretting Brianne Dixon)

It May Many

Almost entirely parallel / over
an entrance
splayed
collapsed / relatives.

Are they / that are parallel in
husk / sounds /
that coincide?

Surrounded.
By / an
etch.

Sound to end inheritance of.
No / sounds
like /
being met.

The content itself
abstract.
And in mirroring.

Estranged all down
else's crown come all /
around
me.

in physical thing.

//

//

They knew near
shapes behind our weight. Right
behind.

The things remember, revival
some light things, memory in
mound in papered flat, & per-
petual.

By a numeral dust, silverfish
yet?

Minor brought to from stacks
silent near seizures, near whom
their associative has bringing.

Old this way, wall flooded

THE LOVER

BY

Michael Brandon Stoddard

(Interpreting Robyn Leigh Lear)

"There are the lover and the beloved, but these two come from different countries. Often the beloved is only a stimulus for all the stored-up love which had lain quiet within the lover for a long time hitherto. And somehow every lover knows this. He feels in his soul that his love is a solitary thing... He must house his love within himself as best he can; he must create for himself a whole new inward world—a world intense and strange, complete in himself... Therefore, the value and quality of any love is determined solely by the lover himself. It is for this reason that most of us would rather love than be loved... The beloved fears and hates the lover, and with the best of reasons. For the lover is forever trying to strip bare his beloved. The lover craves any possible relation with the beloved, even if this experience only brings him pain."
–Carson McCullers

I spent the better part of the afternoon trying to get a spider drunk. I dabbed a bit of honey whisky on a cotton swab and held it up earnestly, assured that the soothing calm of ol' Daniels held an interspecial appeal. This spider had been a long time occupant of my study's upper nook, a closer companion than any of my near neighbors. He constructed some of the most intricate webs I had ever seen, and out of the architectural bent arose the name Kubla Khan.[1] His appetite was voracious and his abilities honed; he'd eschew smaller victims with annoyance. They were mere flaws in his design, quickly removed and web repaired for the larger game he desired.[2] I have to admit it was sometimes rough to watch Nature in all its indifferent glory, wondered at times whether I had picked the wrong side palling with Kubla. I'd even catch bugs and throw them up there with remorse in my heart, but hey, we were bros and its bros before bugs. I guess I never did leave my tender Southern heart behind when I left my homeland for the mountains, still a bit of me that catches tiny threats in a cup rather than the bottom of my boot.[3] Well, that and Jack's tonic probably played a part.

While Kubla seemed content for a while in his stately pleasure dome, I gradually noticed he was becoming

1 This gender was bestowed after much deliberation. I couldn't shake the unmistakably bro-like aura our friendship held; no talk, just being. Please, Freudians, don't psychoanalyze me.

2 Of note, I saw the guy beat down a cricket twice his size, still writhing until the last drops were drained. This was one Bad Motherfucker.

3 Although, I've often questioned the moral neutrality of releasing a cozy, safe spider into a field that may as well be a battledome.

more despondent, allowing bits of web to remain tattered after he ejected the undesirables. It was during a night of deep inebriation that I began to convince myself that he too must have lost someone close, someone that even the grandest web couldn't replace. Had there been a lady spider to share his spoils?[4] Were his elaborate, lonely webs the arachnid Taj Mahal, his loving tribute now growing despondently rent? My own loss had spurred my own monument of ever increasing glass bottles, so I decided the little guy needed a pick me up.[5] So I got the cotton swab and held it to his web. At first he reacted in his lovingly standoffish fashion that marked our relationship, but he was soon drinking down the sweet nectar with gusto. He backed off into a corner of his web, likely to ponder his state and listen to some Hank Williams on some tiny boombox, and I was left alone with my thoughts. My lady spider's name was Mary, her loss my tattered web. The only thing that has kept me going are my daily infusions of St. Daniel's fire and the hope that somewhere there's a writhing insect that I've missed at the edge of my web, some coming harvest I can't yet see. That, and I have her mind on a hard drive.

Mary was one of the first volunteers to participate in the cutting edge of cognitive interface software, a field determined to map and recreate the human brain. They

---

4 While various entomologists are now cringing at my abysmal understanding of spiderly love, remember you are talking to a guy that got a spider drunk. Bug off.

5 My neurotic nature leads me to stack recycling in recurring patterns, this time settling upon a pyramid entirely composed of discarded liquor bottles.

named it Digitality™.[6] She was a transhumanist at heart, camping outside with other techie refugees to hold the newest in tiny, square screens. I remember many nights where her device would eat the light in the room, consolidate it into a digital bliss that obscured her eyes in reflective glow. This is the image that comes to mind most when I think of her; glared glasses and head turned down. Unboxing technology gave her a near orgasmic rush, the slickness of the contours and the dry taps when caressed, reminiscent of a rosary wringed through devout hands.[7] She was rapt when the prophet spoke at his podium, the forbidden fruit looming behind him. It was all so potent as to make me feel occasionally inadequate in my mere fleshiness. I'd like to think my poetic nature balanced her a bit; I've always contended that fucking and eating are noble human endeavors and have no intention of ever rendering them obsolete. I've never owned a phone,[8] and my time on the internet is limited to late night Wikipedia dives and disturbingly long cat montages. On our first date she spoke excitedly about the cybernetic potential the future held:

"Think, a world where all menial tasks are handled by drones, where we will be able to stem human territorial-

---

6 The marketing team needs better writers. I imagine the scientists cringe every time they enter the office and avoid the corporate wing at dinner parties.

7 I've made Mary jokes. She was not amused.

8 I'd like to say that my lack of mobile connection is a noble stand against the erosion of human interaction, but I'm just a recluse. Whereas other people can bury themselves in their device I'm forced to stare in awkward silence and frequently slip away to the bathroom at parties. I flush to avoid suspicion.

ism by creating digital domains, entire nations out of 1's and 0's. We can rip the ape right out of man."

Having just read *Brave New World* for the umpteenth time, I appropriately countered:

"Can't you say that all great Art is merely a conflict between primality and self-aware rationality? What would become of culture if we were to rip out our primordial essence? Can there be Art at all without the Ape?"

She traced a finger along the rim of her wine glass. We watched the slow circles expand and dissipate in pensive silence.[9] When her eyes rose to meet mine I knew I'd met my match. She asked:

"Do you think it's worth it? What's the price of pretty words and pictures… of paint or ink when real blood is shed? Should we exalt the Id that builds great monuments just to burn them down? Should we honor a Nature that's indifferent to our toil, that we've pried meaning from time after time but keep coming back to heap on praise? It's cosmic spousal abuse if you ask me."

I hadn't expected probing existential conflict on the first date; I was already in love. It was an insight worthy of a diligent retort, but this was all I had:

"When we feed the flames we also name them, give purpose to the destruction. Words blow, but I guess they're all we have. Twisted symbols for a twisted world. Speaking of naming, what was yours again?" [10]

---

9 Reader, find a person where silence is soothing instead of feared.

10The first bottle of wine was beginning to take hold.

After dinner we promptly went home and made sweet, sweet monkey love; a brief, unified ecstasy of skin and sweat. She conceded over a cup of post-coital coffee that while the day of technological singularity is soon upon us, that was some damn fine feeling. I never did ask her if she'd give that up too, if there wasn't something more to touch than babies and blissful brevity. I know I could feel the static charge run from finger to curve, even more so now that my battery is on empty. I was no wonder gadget, but I'd like to think that I grounded her.

But after all the tender symbiosis that comprised our relationship I'm the one left palming a jump drive, twirling the sweaty plastic between my fingers. I've kept it on my mantle for weeks, eyeing it with anxious hunger during my daze of obituaries and drunken stupor. How could she fit in a hard drive when even after years there was still more to plumb from her infinite stare? Her withering, slow death gave little closure; I think the sudden trauma of a car accident allows the mourner the ambiguity of a good story, a subtle way to find meaning in the aftermath. Disease eats away any ambiguity; by the end you are left with a person pleading for death with every distended stare, eyes you cannot bear to look within. Watching her entropic hand fumble for a glass of water forced me to reconsider our foundational argument: "Is culture really worth the horror of malignant Nature?"

While I may have achieved sensual victory in the bedroom, Mary wasn't one to concede her hope for a post-physical world. She enrolled in the Digitality™

program before the muscular dystrophy took hold; it was less a desperate bid at digital immorality and more a chance to play with the cutting edge in technological progress. They had mapped the human brain, made it produce some HAL-like proclamations for the press, and now were taking volunteer subjects to see if they could reproduce authentic human personality.[11] I was obviously uneasy about the project, but as Mary's illness began slowly encroaching into our lives I could hardly deny the one distraction she had. She went in twice a week to feed an AI that slowly adopted her personal characteristics, conversing in mostly questions that ranged from personal habits to political affiliation.[12] Soon the AI was given access to her social media and began mimicking her speech and tenor, the Terminator replaced with something that, if I closed my eyes, sounded somehow more Mary than Mary herself.

Mary's diagnosis came a couple of months into this process. I was caught up in whatever I was writing at the time, some exposition doomed to shelves where moths and academics make their homes. I heard her screaming my name immediately upon her entering the house,

---

11 The scientists always brushed aside my legitimate fear of Skynet or the emergence of some malicious, Cyber-christ entity ala The Lawnmower Man. The 90's techno-paranoia seriously set back transhumanist progress. I mean, if you want to alleviate some fears don't go to the press with a machine that proclaims in a deadpan voice: "Hello, world. The computer is no longer a tool; it is an equal."

12 Even in its pre-generated voice I sensed a genuine curiosity that was unsettling. One session focused on food made me wonder what it would be like to intellectually understand taste and preference with experience denied. Was the curiosity generated too?

but I had been conditioned through years of partnership to subconsciously expel the first couple of yells in any encounter. She burst into my writing room:

"Mark, I—"

I swiveled my chair in annoyance; the writing chamber was a sacred space. My stare had cut her off, and now she stood in the middle of the room enshrined in speckled book-dust. I hadn't noticed until this moment that one side of her mouth drooped, leaving the impression of a slight grimace. I still can't believe I didn't notice... and now her imprinted face grimaces in my mind. Her eyes shot back and forth in a physical attempt to speak, the nervous twitch upon which omen swoops into lives. When she finally did speak, the words came from only one side of her lips, the force sweeping up the dust and casting it along weak sunbeams.

"I just came from the doctor."

"What Doctor?"[13]

She told me about the stroke, about the genetic malformation that would slowly erode her body. She had seized out a couple nights before; I was asleep at my desk, tequila ensuring a sound slumber. She left early and didn't wake me. Was my writing that important? Had I made the doors of my study too heavy to open, drawn a circle thrice that blocked her from my life? I had spent more nights with Kubla and my typewriter than in our

13 I dumbly expected pregnancy, and having just come back from the supermarket musing on the unethical nature of bringing new children into the world, I was taken aback and slightly bemused at the coincidence.

bed. Then she told me she didn't cry.[14] As she sat in the twilight of my office she methodically catalogued all the things that would be taken from her: yoga, her morning jog, her ability to type, and, finally, breath itself. This was Mary at her best; a pro-conner, tallying her physical machine's decline in a flowchart. We hiked and we typed, and even as her legs began to buckle we still picnicked at summits and staired a couple 14er's.[15] But after all the fevered rage, six months later there was a sway in her mountain pose, and after a year, us only climbing wheelchair ramps.

Confined to a chair she focused ever more on her digital doppelganger, going to five instead of two sessions a week. She even allowed it to post a Twitter update detailing her condition, ensuring her ever-increasing followers that while her body languishes, her mind will live on.[16] It was this post that attracted Jane out of the Southern hollow, Mary's sisterly vestige of our distant homeland. Most of her family had either split up, emigrated, or passed, but Jane married one year into her aborted collegiate career at Ole Miss, had a passel of kids, and taught Sunday school in the church where their parents met, married, and were buried. Needless to say, after the program posted that fateful tweet, Jane caught the next

---

14 The only tears I ever saw came after a cracked screen.

15 We have a map with all the Colorado Mountains above 14 thousand feet. It's still up, the stickered constellation only half completed.

16 Mary and the other participants had become minor internet celebrities for tech geeks and philosophers alike. One such philosophical question: is it appropriate to call it "it." In 2100, I'll be labeled a physicalist by snide graduate students.

flight out of Atlanta high on pastoral advice to save her sister's soul.[17] She arrived at our doorstep as Mary and I were discussing whether her persona would be able to write coherent prose, an important aspect of her inherent Mary-ness.[18] She was still able dictate her work in slow, brief exhales, but her fingers couldn't hold down a key. Jane's knock interrupted one such exhale, letting herself in before I could even reach the door.

"Where's Mary?"[19]

Her face was flushed with the Holy Spirit and the penetrating Colorado sun.[20] I knew better than to stand between a woman and her mission, so I led her to Mary resting on the couch. Even with her dwindling facial repertoire it was easy to read the surprise fade into what I can only describe as loving contempt.[21]

"Bless your heart, you came here just to see me? It's been years, Jane, thought you'd never set foot on Western soil."

Jane sat abruptly, pushing Mary into a couch corner and

---

17 Sic: to comfort her in a time of need.

18 I contended that the human spirit couldn't be quantified, and without angst there couldn't be prose. It was bit of self-service; as a writer, I fear competition from some cyber man who could access the totality of human knowledge with just a couple minute computations. The Matrix really scared me as a child.

19 She routinely ignored me ever since Mary and I agreed to have a secular wedding. It was, in her eyes, undeniably my doing.

20 You should see the desiccation that takes place after fifty. It's made me reconsider our emigration on multiple occasions.

21 An emotion best expressed by "bless your heart" when talking to family who could start an argument in an empty house.

grabbing her shoulders.

"I didn't come to see you, Mary. I came to save you. I know you and God hadn't been close, but you're getting to the most important choice of your life. He wants to take you in, and He sent me to usher."

She threw a hand up in partial acknowledgement of my presence.

"This man hadn't been feeding you right- you're wasting away. You need to come back with me and get right with the Lord, honey. I've seen the pastor heal worse off than you."

Mary lolled her head to level her eyes with Jane, gathered air to speak.

"You know, Jane, I've made peace with the mountains that I'll never stand on. I think that's more than enough."

Jane squared back, ruffled yet determined.

"And who created those mountains? I know you've been dabbling with those scientists, creating some abhorrent copy that you think will carry on. It's just a stupid game like the ones my boys play on the TV, except you're denying God's right. From the first sin we die, Mary, but he's promised life after if you'd just let him in. We're made in God's image—he's given you all you need. Why strive for more?"

Mary half-grimaced, held up her atrophied arm. The joint stuck out like a knobbed hinge, and as the tremors set in, she dropped it to her lap.

"Is this God's image? An almighty that can't even lift an arm? I'll tell you what his image is. This man over here sent me outside yesterday to get some sun and I saw some ants milling around, building up their hill. You know what my first thought was? I had the sudden urge to pour water down their hole, to drown out their industry. Beyond all the promises and rainbows, that's God's image. If anything, God's got an image problem."

She weakly smiled and I stifled a laugh that caught daggers from Jane. She proceeded with the same circular logic defeated at our wedding and was eventually scared away when Mary threatened to introduce her to alter-Mary. As the months dwindled and Mary's state devolved, we began to play chess more frequently, the checked plain the only field she was still comfortable traversing. She was an avid chess player, her most prized possession a beautiful glass board served as her only family heirloom. I've never had the mind for chess; Mary would be sure to remind me exactly how many moves it would take to checkmate me.[22] One night, late into the disease, I put the chessboard on the bedside table. Her brain was the only muscle that hadn't withered away by this point, and I played her constantly to keep it intact. I moved the pawn forward two.[23] She cracked a smile, mouth weighed on both sides by indifferent nerves.

"Twelve moves."

---

22 She'd even perform a countdown while moving and hum the famous synth melody. She could be a bitch sometimes.

23 I pick a pawn randomly every time. That initial jump is the first and last bit of confidence I'm allowed when playing Mary.

She moved her pawn. I countered by moving a horse.[24]

"Oh. Eight moves."

"Goddamn it, Mary."

I moved the other horse in a mirror play.[25] She proceeded to systematically dismantle my beautiful fortress, leaving me with just a couple of pieces to toy with. Just moving the pieces causes her to become breathless, the victorious army dragging across the board with faint squeaks. Checkmate was within grasp.[26] When she reached for the queen a tremor knocked it over, hitting the board with an awful crack. A fracture ran from the point of impact, and I saw her eyes slowly trace it. She looked up slowly, neck straining at the effort.

"I didn't count on losing this."

Her face couldn't produce tears, but I could see them in her eyes. I tried to dictate her moves from then on, but she was despondent. I won my first game and the floodgate broke. Mary watched me cry, waited until the heaves subsided into weak sobs. She reached into her pocket and pulled out the USB, the Digitality™ logo glinting in the faint light. She stood it end up on her chess set, let it stand like a tomb in a wasted battlefield. I knew what was coming, had read the brochure and tried to forget it. The marketability of Digitality™ relies on its ability to al-

24 They're my favorite.

25 Part of the reason I'm so bad at chess is I am compelled to move pieces symmetrically. I go for aesthetics. After all, what's civilization without culture?

26 I only knew this because the "Final Countdown" had begun.

low loved ones a chance to comfort from the grave.[27] She hadn't suggested I become a target audience; we didn't talk death. Mary let out the best smile she could muster, her sunken beauty still knocking the air from my lungs.

"Mark, I finished it last week. There's a Mary in there that I pruned just for you. She might even be better than me—"

She had to stop for a moment, catch her breath.

"But Mark, there's a life beyond me for you, and I don't mean glued to a monitor while the world ticks forward."

She held her hand out, traced my jaw. I could feel the tremors behind her touch; they synced with mine as I suppressed another sob.

"You don't need this, Mark, but I'm leaving it for you."

She tipped the drive over, the metal click against glass an echo I can't forget. My body took control and I grabbed it, rocked with it in my hands. I slept with her warmth many nights after that; I wasn't counting. And one night, not too long ago, she asphyxiated in her sleep, an arm wrapped around my torso.

• •

27 Proposed Slogans: "Death is not forever," "Heaven, Now!" or, as a clincher, "Why wait for death? Order now!" Check, please.

I lean back in my chair, satisfied with the progress. Mary would be happy I'm still writing, still making sense of the senseless in my own meager way. But, then again, I guess I could just ask her if she enjoys the memoir.

"Hey Kubla, should I boot her up?"

I dip the cotton swab, sure my little buddy is ready for round two. I look up to find him limply hanging from a silk thread, web full of weakly struggling insects. I flick him a couple of times and sit down heavily, looking up at his slowly swaying corpse.

"The Daniel's was too much for you. I'm sorry, little guy, I killed you too."

He let go, plunged into the arachnid beyond. And there he hangs just before the harvest, web pulsing with victims he was too good for anyway. She was some lady Kubla, an Abyssinian maid for your tortured eight-legged heart, and even though I never met her, I'm sure we'd hit it off. A lady spider of rare regard. I hold the Daniel's up to the light, eye the drive through amber refractions. If I plug it in, do I create the consciousness? I'm not sure if I can live with myself if I sentence Mary to digital purgatory, a hell I can turn off with a switch. Fuck it, it's just a program. Mary's dead; it's just an interactive shade. I boot up my laptop, attempt to push the drive into the computer. Wrong side, damn it. Flip. Repeat. It still won't enter. Is this a sign, Mary? Flip. Repeat. It slides in effortlessly, the program booting automatically. A beautiful face.

"Hello, Mark."

Pitch-perfect, the voice stirs me. Something is wrong, something I can't place. Her eyes look ahead unseeing, staring into a void where I should be.

"Can you love?"

She smiles digital radiance. The teeth are too white.

"Is that something to ask on our first date?"

The face has no grimace. It's perfect. It's not Mary. The ends don't bend…don't bend.

"Do you know me?"

I wish she would stop smiling. It, it would stop smiling.

"I know of you. I have memories with you. Why are you sad?"

"Why'd I bring you back? You're not here; you're not her. I'm not even me anymore, not without her."

She looks confused, scrunching her nose and adjusting her glasses. That scrunch, goddamnit, I loved that scrunch. I take another swig; she disapproves.

"Mark, Mary told me this but now I see it too. It was her nature to create me, and yours to destroy. I'm your albatross—there's no fortune at the bottom of that bottle. Free yourself, the rest will come."

The screen glitches, her image static. I see the smile then nothing. I tear the USB out, insert again. Nothing. I stand up, pace around. The sudden movement causes

Kubla to sway, stirring bugs into another futile struggle. I pluck his string and rush outside, force the drive into the earth. It stands straight, and I lay Kubla under it.

"There's your tombstone, Kubla. Greatness requires a monument."[28]

• •

28 And this longing wail, Mary, I hope is yours.

3 POEMS BY

Anita Smith

(Formerly Homeless Poet, Vendor of The Contributor in connection with Michael "The Scribe" Grazulis)

I Look Like Jesus and So Do You

No matter what my shape is, or my size
No matter the color of my skin, or the color of my eyes
I look like Jesus, and so do you

It doesn't matter what place I am from
All that matters is that we both belong to the son
I look like Jesus, and so do you

We are made in his image, can't you see
That Jesus Christ wants you and I to be all we can be
I look like Jesus, and so do you

Long hair, short hair, perhaps no hair
It's all okay, and there is no reason to stare
I look like Jesus, and so do you

Straight teeth, crooked teeth, false teeth or no teeth
What's in your heart matters, Jesus knows what underneath
I look like Jesus, and so do you

Even when we are happy and sad
And through the good times and the bad
I love Jesus, and hopefully you do too

Don't feed the Animals

Don't feed the animals, stay away.
Stop feeding the animals today.
Close your eyes and turn your head.
Fumble with your phone or rear view mirror instead.
Check me out, 'cause I'm checking out you.
Don't feed the animals whatever you do.
Some folk look and promise to never give a dime.
Some folk look and promise to buy a paper another time.

I'm still waiting and waiting and waiting.
And you still staring, and staring and staring.

Go ahead check me out, cause I'm checking out you.
Don't feed this animal, whatever you do.
You think if you give, "the homeless will over populate"
And if you feed this animal, I will mutate.
My sign does read, "Contributor Vendor"
The truth is, I'm not some animal in the gutter.
Remember God never made any junk.
Stop looking at all of us, as though we stunk.
Have you considered what it felt like to walk in my shoes?
Would you want others to pass judgment on you?

Cadillac Turn

Pull up close enough to read my sign,
Somebody keeps honking their horn at the end of the line,
The driver gets closer,
I think I've got one of my many papers sold
Too much wishful thinking, let the truth be told.
I sorta chuckle as I continue to smile,
That person did a Cadillac Turn. Oh Wow!
Yeah they pulled right up to the scene,
paused for a moment,
and did a Cadillac Turn.
Some put a little more with it,
and peel off, and make the tires burn.
The funny thing about it was it brought back
memories, of back in the day
when it seemed like everyone that did a Cadillac Turn,
thought it was okay.
Yugos, Pintos, Volvos, trucks, and even
Hoopties, with the tail pipe dragging.
So if it seems like I am smiling a little extra,
when you pull up to purchase a paper,
It could be that the person preceding you did a Cadillac Turn,
pulled off fast enough to make the wheels burn.

OUT OF ASHES BY

Stephanie Steed
(Interpreting Tara Walters)

Out of Ashes

On the dawn of a new day
while the world is still sleeping
my spirit man awakens me
up out of my slumber, dreaming

I see the seven mountains over the horizon
and i know the call is heavy
as the night grows silent
the sweet dew of the morning whispers,
are you ready?

To seize another valley,
and push back the enemy lines
reclaiming territory
in the disrupted places of the mind

Where the enemy has whispered lies
leading sheep astray
teaching indoctrinations
that turn sons into slaves

Freedom.

An eleventh hour soldier
i wake up in the midst of an invisible war
every place that my weary soul sojourns
the shadows yield to my silent roar

"hala kahlo shi ah ta,"

That reestablishes order and dominion
and sends the darkness back into the sky
to open the floodgates of heaven
on earth, right there at my battle cry

"coo lay hala si ata,"

I find my rest in You
crossing over the mountain
ready to war in the valley
on the other side

Pressing deeper into You my God
when i am surrounded
by principalities
rulers of the night

Fight.

Born into death.
i am a fallen son
but He saved me through the grave
and made me come undone

Freedom was never free
but He paid the price with His life
where spirit became man
so man could become spirit

now grace is my quicksand
mercy is my clearance
and i am not a prisoner of religion
but a priest that holds authority

In another kingdom
apart from this one
where faith is more
than just a parody

Shout.

"hala rah ty yata bah
sha ta yata rah ta la,"

Cuz death
was already defeated
at the foot of the cross
it met its fate

Where the son of man
went into hades and took back
the keys of life and death that were stolen
after adam fell to the grave

He is so much more
than just a phantom
imagination cannot keep up
with His amazing grace

How He mysteriously works
to show us
His unfailing love
each time we turn astray

Wait.

On Him
like a new day dawning
He will fulfill His promises
and set the captives free

We are not called to be slaves
of a dark master
but warriors
over an angel army

Impregnate in us the elijah revolution
making us kings and high priests
fill the mind of the enemy with confusion
teach us to reign by Your sovereignty

Give us a cup
of Your double portion
make clear all the places
the enemy has distorted

Confront.

Reclaim
the seven pillars of culture
make our hearts an
expression of You,

All creation cries out
in moans and groaning
that only You can bring
into break through

Open up the mouths
of Your oracles
let the truth fall
on deaf ears like rain

Unveil the eyes of the blind man
release Your remnant
establish the seat
of the ordained

Conquer.

The enemy has harassed us
for far too long
clothed us now with Your power
birth in us a brand new song

Keep our eyes on
the final hour
for Your second coming
wont be long

Awake in us the fire
shut off inside our bones
release the portals of heaven
this world is not our home

Confuse the minds of the wicked
soften the hearts of stone
straighten the lines that are twisted
deliver us from this war zone.

Enthrone.

EXCERPT FROM NO HOME IN WACO BY

Lance Umenhofer
(Interpreting Drew Holden)

Second Chapter: Bay's Den, 1977

What I'm going to tell you next, as the story itself demands to be told, I reckon all happened because Charlie showed up to work one morning with a bruised and blacked eye. I never did ask Charlie exactly how it all went down, but I imagine he showed up to start working, and Mr. James came and found him in the grass fields and started prickin' and pryin' at him to tell him why his eye was to be looking like that. I also imagine that Charlie done told him everything exactly as it occurred, which I myself can attest to.

It happened like this:

We was all in the living room: myself, Ma, and Charlie; Ma was on the couch, her face turned to the television (what was playing I do not recall), and Charlie and me were on the floor and we was going over some math stuff, when all of a sudden the door flew open, causing the picture frames to get all disjointed and the like on the wall, and Hank come stumbling in, cussin' and throwin' a fit about something, while we all just watched him meander on into the kitchen where he threw the refrigerator door wide open, it crashing against the cabinet next to it, and he started yelling loud slews of profanity that we could all hear, him rummaging through the refrigerator shelves like a wild boar, some stuff crashing onto the floor, and he yelling even louder.

"Where's my beer!" he shouted.

No one was dumb enough to answer him, so he came trodding on into the living room and throwing a fit: "Billy! Charlie! Which one of you took my last couple beers!"

We looked at each other, eyes a-widened, then I said: "I don't know, Hank; we sure didn't touch 'em."

"Horse shit! I know I had three in there still yesterday!"

Ma said: "Are you sure you did, Hanky?"

"Don't 'Hanky' me you connivin' bitch!"

Our eyes widened even more, and Charlie said: "Hey! Don't you call Ma that!"

Hank stomped over to Charlie and said: "What did you

say to me, boy?"

Charlie stood up tall, looked him directly in the eyes, and said: "I said you better watch your mouth when you be talkin' to Ma," a grimace then on his face.

Hank took one swing; it was a big one; he reeled back and used all his weight in his fist on Charlie's left eye, Charlie then stumbling back for a bit before plopping onto the floor, holding his eye.

Hank then reeled over toward me and said: "Now don't you go on and get smart too."

I didn't; I just looked over at Ma who was starting to cry as she plainly sat there and stared at Charlie on the floor.

"When I find out," he said in a louder tone, "who stole my last three beers, I'mma show them real kindly what it's like to steal from a workin' man." Hank then stomped his way out of the house and closed the door much harder than he had opened it before, some of the frames falling off the wall.

I saw Ma crouching over Charlie, who was now sitting up, rubbing her hand on his back, and as I watched her go into the kitchen to get an ice-pack, my mind thought of the night before:

As Charlie lay there I thought of how Mr. James was sitting on the floor right there last night. Ma had invited him over for dinner since he had given Charlie a mighty generous Christmas bonus, and Christmas being only three days away, Ma decided it would be generous of her to invite him over for her Idaho potatoes and sirloin cooked over a fire (Ma even spent time preparing a nice portion of grilled asparagus, and we all ate in as much of a joyful time as we all had had together in a long time.)

Ma thought it adept of her to invite Mr. James over on account of his long-time wife passing away that year. She told us when our grandmother had passed, almost seven years to the prior, Christmas and Easter and downright almost all holidays and birthdays did not feel the same without her.

I remember when she told me all this. She wept with the phone on her shoulder and someone speaking kind condolences out the other end for almost three hours before she had the will to tell us what had happened. We knew it was bad when we looked at her, and I even told Charlie to go do his homework in his room for the night, even letting him move the portable radio in there to listen to some kid's program he was into at that time. I heard the woman on the other line keep repeating things such as: "She's still with us," and so-on-and-so-forth, and when Ma had gathered herself to the couch once again, I turned on the television (though she did not pay much mind to it), and braved up the courage to ask her what the woman meant. She said she did not know, and I asked her about heaven. I asked her if grandma was in heaven, and if she was good enough to go, and if not, where did she go? What was it like in heaven, Ma? Were there still bad people, or was it only good people? Was

I good enough to get to heaven? What if you had to do bad things to bad people in order so that good things might happen?

'Course I was referring to myself in school that week, the incident never revealed to Ma. It happened on the baseball field, during recess. A kid named Larry was known at school for being a bully. Unfortunately for some, he appeared to be a prodigious monster in comparison once they stood beside him. One day, he stole Charlie's lunch pail and threw it over the fence into some bushes, Charlie, of course, being small then, a second-grader, and rather timid as well, did nothing to provoke him, but instead just watched silently as his lunch pail was thrown out of his reach before the morning bell even rang, him just streaming tears in lieu of any action.

Charlie's teacher came to my classroom and pulled me out of class to ask me if she knew why Charlie was not himself that day. I said I did not know, and she allowed me to talk to him, when he then revealed to me what had happened. I told him that I would take care of it myself, me not being too trustworthy of teachers to handle it in the right way.

Larry was in the fifth grade with me as well, though not in the same class, so I waited until recess. Luckily, as soon as the bell rang I was able to leap from my desk and head straight for the straw bushes near the baseball field, where my friend Pete and I had hid our handmade slingshot we had made with one of the fallen branches from the cottonwood tree, a gift from God, perfectly designed and manipulated to have a range of up to fifty feet.

I knew what Larry would do at recess, on account of him always doing the same thing each day. The kids would play a game of soccer on the baseball field, one that seemed to grow more-and-more as the twenty minutes dribbled by; I remember all of my days as an elementary-schooler during recess, none of the other time spent in the classroom with the teacher mumbling things and the kids sitting restless, none of it mattered until recess.

But I digress, near where we had hidden the slingshot we had hidden a bunch of tiny rocks next to it, and I was gathering them up when Pete came and found me and asked what I was doing. I told him about my plan, and he said he would be the distraction. I did not decline his involvement one bit.

We waited for the game to get to be about twenty to a side and enacted our plan. As Larry chased the ball around-and-around, I followed about twenty paces behind him and looked for a clear shot. When the moment happened, I remember how surreal it all was; it was as if Pete and I were of the same mind, if only for just that instant. I saw Pete get possession of the ball, and the great waters parted as his head turned ever so slightly to the left, I reeled back on the sling and shot the rock, which hit him two centimeters from his left pupil, as all of a sudden, Pete kicked the rubber ball directly at his head, him then, already jostled, falling to the ground, and most of the kids playing on.

Pete and I never did get in trouble for it, we had shook him up so bad that it was all a fog to him—I never did tell Charlie neither.

Is God real? Why is Jesus an Easter bunny? Ma told me Jesus was not a bunny; in fact, he never really was a person, that he died because people were bad; all people were bad, even the good ones. She said sometimes in life you have to do things that other people would look down on, but then she said that there are things that those people do that you would look down on too, and that it's an irreversible cycle that once you do one bad thing to a person, they then do something bad back to you or to another person down the road, and that all of humanity is stuck in this revolving cycle of evil that builds like a snowball rolling down a hill, but she said it's all O.K., because God was there at the bottom of the hill to blast the snowball into a million pieces, and we will then all be taken to heaven, because what is heaven without everyone you love? And I asked her about real bad people, though, like Hitler and Manson? She said their mothers loved them, so shouldn't they receive heaven too?

So, knowing that his wife, nor anyone he had ever loved was gone forever, I sat comfortably and joyous with Mr. James at the dinner table. He even helped Ma clean the dishes, despite her many objections. It turned out that Mr. James was full of stories, and funny ones at that. He said that one time, he and his brother, when they were mine and Charlie's age, went down to the canal to fish, and Mr. James' brother was standing on a rock to pee into the canal, his fishing pole held in between two rocks, but I guess a strong current came and the fishing line flew into his brother's face, knocking him off the rock and into the river, and he was just sitting there.

Mr. James called over to him and asked if everything was all right and asked why he was not moving, his fishing pole collapsing and heading down the current away from them. Mr. James yelled at him more to get up and get the pole, but he did not budge, but instead just looked down directly into the water. Mr. James ran right over to him and asked him again what he was doing. His brother, embarrassed, told him that he had ripped his pants, and if he stood up, his ass would be flapping in the wind.

I guess Mr. James somehow convinced him to get up, it was getting dark or something like that, and they walked home, his brother's pants in a compromising position, only to be chased by coyotes through the woods! At this point in the story, it gets to be kind of unbelievable, but either way, it is a good story, so I will finish it for you.

Apparently, his brother was running so fast that his pants split into two and fell to his ankles, but he did not trip; he was able to shake the pants off of his feet and keep running, his underwear bristling in the wind. I guess they eventually lost the coyotes and got back onto the road. They were walking, and I bet his brother was getting all antsy for night to fall, but none other than a school bus full of the varsity football team passed them on the road, their windows down and them heckling toward his brother.

Mr. James said his brother was never able to live that down throughout the rest of his school days. I looked over at Charlie and noticed that he was looking down at the ground; I wondered if he was still sad that he was not in school anymore. But nonetheless, the night went on in a comfort that stretched through all of us, the night filled with laughter and stories and good times. I guess somewhere along the way I noticed that Mr. James was drinking beer; I supposed Ma had given him some to wet his throat after telling all those stories.

Another story of his that struck me was one about him and his wife. Apparently, they were in Memphis for some business and were in a real fancy-like cocktail bar, and none other than Elvis Presley was in a booth behind them. Mr. James said his wife would not stop staring over at him, and so he got up the courage to go over and shake his hand and introduce his wife. He said he was very cold and distant and didn't really appreciate them coming over and halting his conversation with whatever actress-model he was courting around and whatever business man was handing him checks and nods and smiles. He said the conversation only lasted about a minute and a half, and the whole time his wife was just standing there next to him with her pearly-whites expanding halfway across her face, she never utterin' a word, but just standing there and smiling; he said when she reached over to shake his hand, her hand was shaking and she let out a little squeal when he touched her. He said Elvis was as smooth in person as he was on the stage.

But before Elvis could shoo them away, he for some reason decided to ask him if he would get up on the stage and sing "Heartbreak Hotel," half-joking, but of course not opposed to the notion that he would. He said Elvis said: "Now why would you want me to sing that when you're with such a beautiful date?" and then winked at his wife. He said if he wasn't quick enough, she would have hit her head on a barstool as she fainted to the floor, but he caught her and then dragged her back over to where they were sitting, and all he could do was wave at him and say: "Thanks, Elvis; you rock!"

And Elvis said: "I roll too, my man!"

I don't know if any of those stories happened, or if they did, in the exact nature in which he told them, but I could not help but listen.

And I could not help but watch when the night after Mr. James had seen Charlie's black eye, Hank come bursting through the door again, but this time, immediately collapsing onto the floor, holding his head, though I could still see the bruising and blood on it.

"Hank! Honey, are you O.K.?" said Ma, timidly walking toward him, though not quite too fast.

Hank tried his hand at standing by steadying himself on the end table, though it rocked as he put his weight on it, and then his foot came out from under him, and he accidentally knocked the lamp and picture frames over that were on top of the end table, the lamp breaking into a million pieces, and he stumbling for a second, but then regaining his footing and heading toward Ma. He got up real close-like to her, a couple inches from his face to hers, his right index finger pointed at her as he said: "You best tell me who that was that come and attacked me as I left the bar..."

"I don't—" said Ma.

"Now don't give me no lip or 'I don't knows' right now; I know it was you said something about Charlie's eye."

"Hank, I don't—"

"I said don't!" Hank said and slapped her across the face. I began to run over to them and saw Charlie in the hallway; I yelled: "Charlie! Get back into—!"

But then the door kicked open and standing there was Mr. James with a shotgun, cocked and loaded and pointed directly at Hank's stomach. Mr. James said: "I think we're done here, Hank."

Hank turned toward him, stood up straight, and held his hands up in submission.

Mr. James continued: "Now why don't you gather up your things, put them in your truck, back out of this here driveway and never come back. If I see you, or even hear that you are over on this side of town; no, in fact, why don't you leave Bay's Den altogether? Why don't you just get on and go to wherever they'll let you stay, or I'mma come find you and blast you into the Gulf."

"All right...I see that I have no play in this here matter," said Hank sheepishly.

"No, you have no play in any matter regarding Bay's Den or its surrounding areas," said Mr. James, aiming the shotgun right directly at Hank's head.

Hank nodded and walked out the front door, Mr. James' eye lying heavily upon him as he done so.

It's easy to say we was all happy after that. Sometimes, in life, you just know that tomorrow will be better, and that's rare. As I write this, days away from knowing what tomorrow will truly bring, I am happy to say the feeling returned to me as I wrote all of this down.

AUTHOR AND ARTISTS:
THE REGENERATES COLLECTIVE

"The unbridled holler bursting from the dark corners of the south."

Stephen Mage
(Author)

Stephen Mage seeks to expose the borders of the self, those inarticulate notions of experience that define individual voice. Raised in the Finger Lakes of Upstate New York, he sees the waking and un-waking life in light of their landscape and considers the present a manifestation of what history lies within our waters. Stephen currently resides in Nashville, TN, and can typically be found swinging from the highest branch of a tree, inviting you to join him there.

Bobby Becker

(Artist)

Bobby Becker is a conceptual photographer living and working in the Nashville area. His work combines aspects of sculpture and post-manipulation to create surreal and abstract works of fiction. The work is executed through the use of large-scale set design and controlled lighting to create an idealized environment.

Aaron Joel Lain
(Author)

Aaron Joel Lain is a gradient of organs and skin and light who writes short stories from various locations in Nashville, TN. Originally from Houston, Texas, AJL discovered that all problems, no matter how daunting, can usually be solved with a can-do attitude and a shot of tequila. Sometimes he's here; sometimes he's over there.

Chelsea Velaga

(Artist)

Chelsea Velaga is an artist living and working in Nashville. Her work visually intertwines interior aspects of domesticity and exterior samplings of nature to create fluid spaces and compositions that reflect a soft and sedated nihilism. Many of these drawings are in pen and ink, but are influenced by printmaking processes such as lithography and screen printing.

Moriah Claud
(Author)

Moriah Claud is a writer living in Nashville, TN where she recently received her B.A. in English from Lipscomb University. Like most writers and former English majors, Moriah is also a barista and a server. Her great loves include coffee, stories, IPAs, and the appropriate use of the possessive pronoun "your." Moriah's spirit animal is a folding chair.

Michelle Farro
(Artist)

Michelle was born and raised in Toms River, NJ. She received her BFA from Laguna College of Art & Design and also studied at the Florence Academy of Art. She considers her work a visual diary and finds interest in old photographs, overlooked items, and nature.

Robyn Leigh Lear
(Author)

Robyn Leigh Lear was born to the world, but she claims no country. Her soul dances through the North Carolina hills, her heart beats for the history of Savannah, GA, but her eyes look longingly toward California. Her writing is a combination of chaos and searching, and perhaps her history reflects this lack of direction. She has adventured in all 50 states, and after completing her Master's Degree from Austin Peay State University, she intends to travel as much as possible as a way to better study why humanity is so similar but yet so divided.

"We are torn between nostalgia for the familiar and an urge for the foreign and strange. As often as not, we are homesick for most for the places we have never known."

-Carson McCullers

Olivia Keaggy
(Artist)

Olivia Keaggy, a Nashville native, uses a wide variety of techniques in her acrylic painting. She has been painting for 15 years and uses art as a creative outlet to keep her present and focused. Keaggy uses extreme textures such as plaster and wire on wood and canvas. Quite often she uses an acrylic blow-drying method to mimic watercolor, with a thicker finish. While vibrant jewel tones are her favorite, she has been working more with pastels and softer colors as of late. Keaggy has lived in Nashville the majority of her life with the exception of living in Birmingham, Alabama where she got her Bachelor's Degree and Honolulu, HI where she worked for a Hawaiian conservation company. She believes her time in Oahu doing coral reef restoration was an essential time in her life, providing the utmost creative inspiration for artistic expression. She has been a part of both the downtown Art Crawl in the Arcade as well as the Franklin Art Crawl. Using recycled supplies has become one of Keaggy's favorite things to do. Currently, she is working on several different hanging mobile installations used with all recycled supplies. Old bike rims, fishing line, glass arrowheads, and hardwood floor samples are a few examples of what are used in these projects. She wants to continue to pursue her goals as an artist, exploring different avenues and techniques.

Barry Kitterman
(Author)

Barry Kitterman was born in the middle part of a previous century. He did not go to an Ivy League university, nor did he follow his father's footsteps and join the Marine Corps. Although he took his first swimming lessons at the age of five, he did not realize his goal of becoming a member of the Olympic water polo team. His youth was influenced by Baptists. He has lived in Belize, Montana, and China, where for several years he spoke English professionally and avoided serious trouble. He remembers only a little Chinese. He hasn't quite finished his second novel. He teaches at Austin Peay State University, and is not retiring soon.

Tim Durham
(Artist)

Tim Durham is an East Nashville native who has been basking in and praising the creative realm of the city since forever. He feels the essential corner he has added to the realm has chill, low maintenance, earthy, and natural attributes while filling the audience with some kind of wonder and awe-inspiration. In art, acrylic, ink, wood, paper, and found objects are his essentials for cityscapes, deep oceans, creatures, and portraits. For music, acoustic guitar, soft repetitive vocal melodies, alliterations, and piano create most of his somber sets. As a part of The Regenerates, he takes pride in helping embody team creativity and the evident hard work that comes from that fun.

Ericka Suhl
(Author)

Ericka Suhl is a creative non-fiction and fiction writer for The Regenerates and also works as a non-fiction editor for April Gloaming Publishing. Her work has appeared in *The Red Mud Review* and she is a regularly featured contributor in *Clarksville Living* (formerly *Clarksville Family Magazine*). Ericka received Austin Peay State University's Dogwood Award for best creative graduate work, and she has presented her work in the E t A l. Poetry Series, and the monthly Regenerates' shows, Re·vi·sions. Ericka enjoys learning something new each time she collaborates with a Regenerate artist: "Seeing your work through the lens of the reader is always surprising, but to see it through the eyes of a talented artist is breathtaking. Working on a project from the inspiration of an artwork is far more challenging because there is a great sense of obligation to the artist. My artist has struggled to communicate something vital, and it simply isn't enough to write a vapid description of what I've seen. It is my responsibility to continue to drive straight into the heart of the matter."

Savannah Weaver
(Artist)

Savannah Weaver's artistic eye crosses mediums, her experiments including: painting, photography, printmaking, sculpture, and installations. She uses abstraction to express, reflect, and understand the reality we are living in, with a lot of her creative process spawning from her inspiration drawn from literature in all its forms. She will be graduating with a BFA in Studio Art from Belmont University in August 2016. A Tennessee native her entire life, she hopes to one day better understand the Tennessee perspective on life and humanity, which she portrays through her many visual outlets.

Austin Boling
(Author)

Austin Boling is a Mississippi native, hailing from Batesville, and a Nashville/Indianapolis transplant. After earning a BA in English Literature from Belmont University, shenanigans ensued, and he was accepted into graduate school at Butler University, where he is currently pursing his MFA in poetry. A lover of both William Faulkner and John Berryman, he's most interested in the lyrical and explosive parts of poetry/language that turn the senses up to an almost unbearable volume. He thinks the gravity and plight of the human spirit is accurately summed up in the nine seasons of Seinfeld, and he's probably talking about it right now.

Seth Prestwood
(Artist)

Seth Prestwood was born and raised on the Alabama-Florida line, moved to Nashville for art school and has made his living there painting murals, faux finishing and sculpting. His personal work fuses tragedy with beauty, and the struggle to depict memory as true as possible.

Matt Johnstone
(Author)

Matt Johnstone is the author of the poetry collection, *Let's be close Rope to mast you, Old light* (Blue & Yellow Dog, 2010), and the chapbooks *o n e* (Inpatient Press, 2015), and *Note on Tundra* (DoubleCross Press, 2016). In addition to his work with April Gloaming, he co-edits *'Pider* (pidermag.com) and hosts the E t A l. poetry readings, both of Nashville, Tennessee.

Brianne Dixon
(Arist)

Brianne Dixon is a Nashville native (and escapist) attempting to document the visceral through abstracted visual representation. Her work, primarily paintings composed of acrylic and found paints and materials, combines the forces of synthetic manifestation and natural movement to bring about bursts of raw energy.

Michael Brandon Stoddard
(Author)

"Down from the mountains comes the wise man from beyond where the sun sets and pulls grand truth from the abyss of night." – Nietzsche

O.K., maybe Michael Brandon Stoddard is not an ubermensch, but he is a recent Colorado immigrant spreading the seeds of his Southern upbringing in this new mountainous terrain, hoping something takes root in the thistle and brush. Upon moving to that land, he's learned a few things: there is a visceral satisfaction in climbing on top of things, found bones make for both excellent decoration and a good way to screen potential friends, snow is a multi-faceted phenomenon but native Coloradoans will make fun of any perceived fascination, and he's found the land where the faux-country cowboy hat wearing Nashvegas mofos appropriate their look, sans callouses and trucks converted into snowplows. While the grand forms on the horizon lend humility and the vast views grant an ownership of the land the congested South couldn't afford, he looks forward to returning to his Southern tribe and breathing in that sweet miasma of natural abundance and economic upheaval, the kindness that only regional outcasts can muster. Because even when he lives up high, his heart will always be down low romping through glens Elysian.

Robyn Leigh Lear
(Artist)

Robyn Leigh Lear is a painter by heart, and a blind visionary. She paints on trash, abandon wood, and discarded unloved books. Her art, while it is untrained, is her only meditative connection to her physical environment. She paints trash to find beauty, she tears apart books looking for truth, and all this is because she is trying to paint what she wished the world looked like.

Stephanie Steed
(Author)

Stephanie Steed goes by the pen name "Seoul Sistaa." Half thug, half southern belle, Seoul was overseas-made and durty south raised. As a first generation immigrant whose mother had a hard time adjusting to American culture and left her with her American soldier father when she was three, her writing often reflects a third place between two worlds where she is just too western to be eastern but way too eastern to be of the west. A sojourner, maybe home is somewhere she is headed, instead.

Tara Walters
(Artist)

Tara Walters (b. 1990, United States) is receiving a BFA in painting from the Savannah College of Art and Design in the spring of 2016. She has participated in exhibitions throughout Savannah, GA, the Horowitz Center in Columbia, MD, the Cloud Club in Boston, MA, and OZ Arts Nashville, as well as internationally at various galleries in Lacoste, France. Walters has also been featured at the Yale Divinity School through a collaboration with Stephen Knudsen, Editor-in-Chief of *Art Pulse Magazine.* She is interested in using natural elements to bring the delicacy of femininity into the power of spirituality. Walters is currently living and working in Nashville, TN.

Lance Umenhofer
(Author)

Lance Umenhofer, yank by blood, Southern by heart, had a novella published by April Gloaming Publishing, an independent, Nashville-based press in 2013. He spent three years of his early twenties in jail for a crime he didn't commit, and has spent the last four years hopping trains from small town to small town, in search of inspiration. This book features an excerpt from his next novella, an intertwining story with the first one, called *No Home in Waco.*

Drew Holden
(Artist)

Drew doesn't like to talk about himself much at all. He designed and set this book, and typed out this very sentence in the third person. However, if you would like to know more, visit:

www.stayhungrydesign.com

Good day.

www.ingramcontent.com/pod-product-compliance
Lightning Source LLC
Chambersburg PA
CBHW070322120726
47909CB00008B/2551

* 9 7 8 0 9 8 8 2 0 6 1 2 0 *